HOW TO CROSS THE STARTING LINE

Also, by Jefferson Noël

Powerful Presenting: How to Overcome One of the Nation's Greatest Fears

Contact Me:

www.jeffersonnoel.com
Instagram: @jeffnoelspeaks
Twitter: @jeffnoelspeaks
jeffnoelspeaks@gmail.com

HOW TO CROSS THE STARTING LINE

JEFFERSON NOËL
JEFFERSONNOEL.COM

GO!

How to Cross the Starting Line

Copyright © 2019 by Jefferson Noel. All rights reserved under International and Pan-American Copyright. No part of this book may be used or reproduced in any form or by any electronic or mechanical means, including information storage and retrieval systems, without permission in writing from Jefferson Noel, except in the case of brief quotations embodied in critical articles or reviews.

ISBN: 9780999296141 (Paperback)

ISBN: 9780999296158 (eBook)

www.JEFFERSONNOEL.com

Printed in the United States of America

DG5050A0001

To those who crossed the starting line before me…

To those who overcame great struggle…

To those who started despite fierce opposition…

To those who overcame their own insecurities…

To those who are hungry for success…

To those who genuinely seek the well-being of others…

To those who sacrifice their time for others…

To those who gift their talent and treasures…

To those who have the fruits of the spirit…

To those who paved the way through the wilderness…

To those who lifted as they climbed…

To those with an open heart and mind…

To those who shine their light in the darkness…

To those who give selflessly…

*To those whose **LOVE** has no bounds…*

Thank you!

Actiophil ['akSH(ə)-fil']

Noun

1. a genuine person who loves to take action towards a purposeful outcome.

Contents

Author's Note	1
Actiophil	5
SECTION 1	**11**
The One-Inch Wall	13
Fear	18
Laziness	31
Delusion Of Perfection	41
Unhealthy Relationships	53
Negative Thinking	73
Excuses	85
Ignorance	97
Success	105
SECTION 2	**117**
Your Greatest Resource is Your Passion	119
Filter Your Energy through Your Value System	125
Power Steps vs Baby Steps	127
The Mosquito Mindset	131

Risk is the Currency of Success	135
Why Matters Most	139
The January 1 Effect	143
Forty is Not Always Greater Than Ten	147
Playoff Mode	153
Big is Not Always Greater Than Small	157
When to Say *NO* and Know When to *GO*	163

SECTION 3 — 167

Never Cross the Starting Line With	169
Lines to Never Cross	179
5 Reasons They Don't Want You to GO	191
5 Reasons to GO	199
1 Reason to Never Stop	207
Acknowledgements	*213*
Endnotes	*215*

Author's Note

I am no stranger to failure.

I was in a "magnet program" called BEAM (Biomedical and Environmental Advancement Program) when I was a student at North Miami Beach Senior High School. That program had the brightest, most astute students, and I was never the "smart kid" in class. One could argue that I was even unmotivated and ungifted. I fell asleep (literally) every day when I came to class. The times I managed to stay awake, I was an average student at best. Most of my classmates would have described me as apathetic toward education and headed toward a shaky future.

After high school, I enrolled at Miami-Dade College, where I lasted one year before dropping out. At the tender age of eighteen, I started a business called Noel's Healthy Living that stood on one of the busiest streets in Miami. Our goal was to better the health of our community through selling healthy drinks and snacks. Unfortunately, I had drained the few resources my parents had in order to lift Noel's Healthy Living off the ground. To my dismay, I failed within four months. In early August of 2013, I shut off the lights and locked the doors, never to open them again. That was a crushing disappointment.

Six months later, four friends and I started a project called "Black Mask 6," where we created replicas of a black mask LeBron James had worn during a pivotal basketball game. We racked up an incredible number of hours preparing over a thousand masks. We aimed to sell the masks at an upcoming Miami Heat basketball game. If we sold all the masks, the profit, we calculated, would add up to around $4,000 for each person. As fate would have it, we only made a total of $110, and two of my friends were detained by Miami-Dade Police. Apparently it was illegal to sell products in downtown Miami without a proper license. They shut us down, and we trudged home with over a thousand black masks in our possession.[1]

Thankfully, my story did not end there. Today, having begun successful businesses, I can proudly say, "I am not the failures of my past."

---

[1] More on this story and its significance later in book.

But first, a bit about my education. I went back to school and graduated with an associate's degree from Valencia College in Orlando, Florida. I then pursued an education at Florida International University (FIU). While at FIU, I served as the Senator of Communications and Journalism, Graduate Senator, Speaker Pro Tempore of the Senate, and President of the student government. When I graduated with my bachelor's degree, the President of FIU, Mark B. Rosenberg, nominated me as a Distinct World's Ahead Graduate. On the day of my graduation, I released a book entitled *Powerful Presenting: How to Overcome One of the Nation's Greatest Fears*. I started a social organization called Barbershop Speaks, where I hosted intelligent discussions inside barbershops and beauty salons on subjects impacting the community. While doing everything mentioned above, I wrote the book you are holding in your hands right now. Despite all my setbacks and shortcomings, I was unafraid to cross the starting line.

Failure is part of what makes me human. Running toward the manifestation of my ideas is part of what makes me phenomenal. I am successful because I can drink the poison of failure without losing the motivation to move forward. Can you?

Dear reader, that is the purpose of GO. I want to help the college dropout develop enough courage, strength, and strategies to go back and finish school. The couple struggling in their marriage will start afresh and embark on the beginning of a new journey. To the private citizen considering running for office in a local election, this is for you. The assembly line worker who has figured out how to increase productivity but does not know the steps to bring those thoughts to fruition will know what to do after reading this book. The single father of four who works fulltime but wants to build an app will understand how to launch.

Many people never reach the finish line because they have not crossed the starting line. Lao Tzu, an ancient Chinese philosopher, and writer, said, "A journey of a thousand miles begins with one step."[1] Yet, what is not commonly taught is that the first step is always the most difficult. For that reason, saying "I have an idea" is easier to say than "I have a plan." The journey ahead of you will not be easy. Trust me, I have experienced loss and disappointment too many times to count. In the words of the social activist and novelist Langston Hughes, "Life for me ain't been no crystal stair."[2] Success does not belong to those who wait around for an opportunity to come knocking. Triumph is only available for the person who decides to GO!

Actiophil

When envisioning success, some people think of a stable career, the car of their dreams, the ideal relationship, healthy retirement, lengthy friendships, a vacation in the tropic islands, and so on. For others, success is traveling the world without limits. Yet another group of people views success as tackling some of the world's most pressing issues, like access to water, mass poverty, and unrighteous wars. Addressing those problems would be major achievements. However, there is a profound difference between those visions and reality.

Most people never cross the abyss to the fulfillment of their innermost desires. Instead, they settle in the comforting arms of small victories. Whether you realize it or not, each person is kept afloat by regularly experiencing a measure of success. Everyone has small victories every day. The bare fact that you are alive is an accomplishment. Since creating a program to help homeless people reintegrate into society is hard, many people with that vision would change their aim to simply providing a roof over their head. Or maybe getting a bachelor's degree is a large step for many folks to take, so they simply wave the banner of victory with their high school diploma.

People who settle with a low-bar victory have the "exist to survive" mentality. That way of thinking will prevent many such people from crossing the starting line toward the "ideal" life. If you're one of those people, this book will help you change that mindset. There is no reason to abide in the land of minor goals. Extraordinary efforts lead to great celebration.

At every FIU graduation ceremony, President Rosenberg highlights three "World's Ahead" graduates; these are students who "exhibit outstanding perseverance, intelligence, and personal strength during their time at FIU."[3] Obtaining a degree is a challenge by itself. But coupling the degree process with deep personal struggle and/or unique innovation makes the accomplishment "world's ahead."

In a recent graduation ceremony, the president of the university highlighted (let's call her) Jamie Espina as a World's Ahead graduate. In 1997, Jamie Espina lost her husband and father of their four children to cancer. Living in New York at the time, she decided to pack up and move with her children to Miami to be closer to her family. Nine years later, she was diagnosed with cancer and put her dream of getting a college degree on hold. When she lost her job in 2011, she finally decided the time was right to go back to school, so she enrolled at FIU. Four years later, she received a degree in International Relations.

Espina's situation was toilsome. But she was driven to cross the starting line despite her circumstances. Unfortunately, most people do not have the same drive as Jamie Espina. Her tenacity is rare and should be admired.

This world is full of good people who have great intentions but don't execute them. If a tree was planted for every person who desired to "get something done" but in actuality did nothing, the world would be a forest. People who neglect their purpose and never deviate from the status quo are rarely remembered. Their names are not placed in the history books, because their contributions to society were minimal at best. Sometimes, their own family two generations later didn't know they existed.

It is important to note that not all people want to be remembered; some simply want to exist. That is their prerogative, but if you want to influence society and etch your name on the stone walls of time, you are in the right place. By reading this book, you have already surpassed the majority of people on the quest to cross the starting line. Thus, for the rest of this book, I will refer to you as an *Actiophil* (my newly coined word). *Actio* is Latin for action. *Phil* is Greek for love. Hence, *actiophil* means "a genuine person who loves to take action toward a purposeful outcome." Becoming an *actiophil* does not require excessive wealth, public recognition, or accolades; all you need is a renewed mind and a commitment to move forward despite fears. Fruition exists at the crossroads of your desires and action.

Taking action might not result in fame. Your name might never appear in the newspapers or on CNN. You might lose money trying to achieve what you hoped for. That is the truth. But consider the alternative. Would you rather live your whole life wondering "What if?" You do not want to be the person on the couch with your shirt stained with Cheetos, watching a commercial, and saying, "Wow! I had that idea twenty years ago. If only I had gone for it, then maybe…"

Such statements do not come out of the mouth of *actiophils*. If they do, that is because their energy was focused on another task that would bring fulfillment if realized. I want you to break past the starting line, not because crossing the finish line will be inevitable but because you will never reach it if you don't start.

Why Become an Actiophil ?

My father was born and raised in Haiti. On the totem pole of power and influence, he and his family were near the bottom. From adolescence to adulthood, no one expected anything positive to come from his life. Sure, he had potential, but who doesn't? Late in his teenage years, he had a decision to make: he could either stay put and follow in footsteps leading to complacency or he could chart his own path and embark on new opportunities. Fortunately, he chose the second option.

As a teenager, my father left his dad's home and jumped on a boat with strangers to come to the United States. My dad crossed the starting line. That scary decision led him to meet my mom at a technical school in Miami seven years later. They married and had three sons and one daughter. If my dad were not an *actiophil*, you would not be reading this book right now. He would have robbed you and the thousands of people of the knowledge shared in this book.

Becoming an *actiophil* is not a birthright. It is a decision. When you look at the portrait of your life, do you see an oasis or a desert? When you examine your motivation and determination levels, do you see emptiness or fortitude? As you lie on your bed at night and think about tomorrow, do you feel hopeful or hopeless? If any of your responses to these questions are negative, fear not. Change is on the horizon. As Victor Frankl, neurologist and Holocaust survivor put it, "When we are no longer able to change a situation, we are challenged to change ourselves."[4] Frankl went on to write, "Everything can be taken from a man but one thing: the last of the human freedoms—to choose one's attitude in any given set of circumstances, to choose one's own way."[5] Whether or not you become an *actiophil* will be determined by your attitude and decision to choose what you love over what you tolerate.

I am a firm believer that every individual life has intrinsic worth and value. Our worth is not determined by what we have, who we know, or how far we go. **We enter into this world with value that surpasses any unit of measurement.** As an *actiophil*, you do not cross the starting line to become valuable. Instead, you cross the starting line to bring the value already inside you to the outside world. You have the power inside of you to shine your everlasting light to the dark corners of this earth. Your intrinsic value remains whether you cross the starting line or not. But for the sake of you making a calculated march toward fulfillment and destiny, I encourage you to *GO*!

SECTION 1

The One-Inch Wall

Starting a journey to the finish line is daunting. The space between your present situation and the starting line is often the most difficult space to overcome. Most people have spent more time moving an inch than others have taken to travel one hundred miles. Through my short time on this earth, I have found that stagnancy is akin to digression. The longer you wait to cross the starting line, the further away the finish line becomes. Everything you've ever hoped or wished for is on the other side of the starting line. If you want the picture in your mind to become reality, you must *GO*.

I must confess, however, that it's not that simple. Best-selling author Eric Thomas says it perfectly: "Success is never on discount! Greatness is never on sale!"[6] If maintaining a marriage was easy, there would be a much lower rate of divorce. If becoming a millionaire was easy, no one would be driving a 1997 Nissan Altima with 180,000 miles on it. If getting a degree was easy, a bachelor's degree would be as valuable as a participation trophy. No, these feats are not easy. Whoever says these accomplishments are simple is either trying to sell you something or wants to see you fail.

When you are standing face-to-face with the starting line, you will always encounter a barrier. Regardless of who you are or where you come from, achieving something that is phenomenal is not easy. All decisions are made in the mind. Whether they are split-second decisions or more deliberate ones, a mental process takes place before every action. The difference between whether you GO or stay put is not the obstacle in the way but your determination, fortitude, and will to break that roadblock. Even Dr. Martin Luther King had nightmares, but he chose to live his dream. I want you to do the same.

On December 16, 2017, I graduated from Florida International University with a bachelor's in communications. On that same day, I released my first book, *Powerful Presenting: How to Overcome One of the Nation's Greatest Fears*. To merge two of those major accomplishments on the same day was extraordinary. In the minds of those who attended the graduation celebration/book release, the double feat was revolutionary. To this day, people are praising me for those achievements. Although I am grateful for their acknowledgment, I recognize that they can do the same thing. Literally. Nothing I have done has required any superpowers, deep connections, or Einstein's mind. I am simply a young Haitian-American millennial who understands the importance of crossing the starting line.

My intention is for you to build the courage to start and experience the joy of finishing. The glories of tomorrow will never come unless you endure the struggles of today. James, the brother of Jesus, wrote in James 1:2-4, "Consider it pure joy, my brothers and sisters, whenever you face trials of many kinds, because you know that the testing of your faith produces perseverance. Let perseverance finish its work so that you may be mature and complete, not lacking anything."[7] Regardless of your religious affiliation or stance, I find these wise words to be a universal truth.

> *The glories of tomorrow will never come unless you endure the struggles of today.*

I will be the first to say that perseverance is difficult. Many people choose to be passive in order to avoid the pain of enduring. People prefer conditioning their mind to be comfortable in a tiny box rather than struggling forward in an open world. If that is your mindset, this book will be of little help. You need a book on *The Negative Effects of Complacency* to recondition your thinking to be as a child so you can begin to dream again about limitless possibilities. However, if you're ready to be an *actiophil*, this book is for you!

The distance between you and the starting line is not empty space. An invisible one-inch wall prevents you and so many others from crossing the starting line. There is a journey before the journey. That one-inch wall contains large, sturdy, and intimidating blocks that prevent people from moving forward. That wall is built with bricks of fear, laziness, unhealthy relationships, negative thinking, excuses, ignorance, delusion of perfection, and even success. This one-inch wall prevents you not only from moving one inch to cross the starting line but also from seeing the finish line. (See Figure 1:1)

Figure 1:1

Breaking down those large bricks is difficult, but it is certainly not impossible. Depending on who you are, Fear and Excuses may be large bricks for you but small ones for someone else. Maybe you are not lazy, but you have not crossed the line because of unhealthy relationships. If that one large piece of unhealthy relationships would come crumbling down, you could easily step over the other bricks and cross the starting line.

During the rest of this section, we will dissect the wall brick by brick. Although this wall is only one inch thick, it seems impenetrable, unbreakable, and impossible to get past. This wall has been in front of you far too long, and it is time for it crumble.

FEAR

When I was younger, the only thing scarier than having a lot of strangers in my house was being at home by myself. Have you ever been in your room alone? Maybe watching TV or doing some work and you hear a noise inside the house…when you know you are the only one home? That scares me! *That sound could be the washing machine or maybe a burglar*, I always think. This has occurred plenty of times. Whenever it happens, I rush to lock my door, flip off the lights, and stay as quiet as possible until I hear another noise. I begin thinking rapidly about whether all the doors are locked or if someone left a window open. Being in those situations of paranoia is terrible because if I step out and actually scope out the situation, I could potentially lose my life. But if I hunker down in my room, the burglar has probably already heard me and will come and eliminate me. Therefore, I choose to remain locked in my room with a makeshift weapon.

This experience is the same one many people have when it is time for them to start. Instead of taking off and breaking past the starting line, they curl into a ball of fear, not knowing what they will find on the other side. This is what I call "The Home-Alone Effect. This occurs when a small inconvenience causes you to retreat and/or remain in a state of paralysis.

In December 2013, I made a decision to move to Orlando. My goal was to uproot myself and get planted in a new field. I wanted to expand my horizons and challenge myself beyond what I thought I was capable of. This was a daring decision because I made it before I developed a cost-benefit analysis. Throughout the process of preparing to leave, many small setbacks occurred that could have thrust me into a state of stagnancy.

During that time, I was working two jobs: at the Juice Spot in Brickell, Miami, and at the Miami Sheraton Hotel as a Valet/Bellman. As a valet, I made a lot more money than the other job, given the services we offered and the money we made through tips. Unfortunately, a couple of days after I decided to move, unbeknownst to the valet company, I got transferred to a new hotel—The Holiday Inn. The place was a nightmare. The foot traffic was significantly less and the number of cars using valet at the hotel was minimal. In contrast, the Sheraton was stationed next to Miami International Airport, where the people we picked up tipped generously. This new hotel did not have that service, and my finances suffered because of it. In addition, The Holiday Inn did not provide lunch for employees, unlike the Sheraton.

The amount of money I made decreased by around 95 percent within one week. Literally. If I had fallen victim to the Home-Alone Effect, I would have taken this as a sign to abandon my plans to move out of my parents' house. The transfer of hotels caused me to have less money to save for the big move. Despite this drastic change, however, I did not retreat to "comfortability."

As I mentioned in the Author's Note, my friends and I started a pop-up business called Black Mask 6. We crafted over a thousand black masks to replicate a black mask Lebron James had worn in a pivotal basketball game. Our goal was to sell the mask in front of American Airlines Arena to Miami Heat fans. We planned on making $4,000 per person. Each of us put in an ungodly amount of hours into making this a possibility. I was especially excited because this was a month before the big move. Unfortunately, we failed. We only made a total of $110, and two of my friends were detained by the police. At that point, I could have decided to postpone the big move, but I didn't. I refused to allow a little noise disguised as a burglar prevent me from crossing the starting line. I refused to fall victim to the Home-Alone Effect.

The range of fears that can trigger immobility is wide. These fears keep people on a leash, restraining them to the misery of their own comfort. Fear grips them in a field of green grass while they secretly desire to play in the oasis of flowers, trees, and fruits.

My life changed when I became terrified of being safe. *I have learned to embrace fear as an inevitable consequence of yearning for greatness.* Therefore, I seek not to limit fear but to instead work to increase my bravery and courage. Starting a business is scary. Moving to a new city is scary. Applying for the upper-division position at your job is scary. Applying for an Ivy League University is scary. Submitting a proposal to the city for a renovation project is scary. Learning a new language can be scary. But more terrifying than any of these is lying on your bed at the age of eighty-five and asking, "What if?"

At this point, given that you are an *actiophil*, you probably feel stuck between a rock and a hard place. You deeply desire to start, but you have legitimate fears preventing you from doing so. Here are some good solutions:

Use Your Fear

Fear has power.

Do you believe fear is objectively bad? I hope not. Part of the reason why you are alive today is not only because of love but also due to fear. I have three siblings—an older brother (David) and sister (Makisha), and a younger brother

(Anderson). Anderson has Down syndrome and Attention Deficit Hyperactivity Disorder (ADHD)—learning disabilities that cause him to require more attention than the average person. As a result, his life can be in danger without him knowing it. Although we teach Anderson continuously to look both ways before he crosses the street, he crosses without looking. That is dangerous. Growing up, we had a fear he would wander out the house and get hit by a car. Consequently, my parents purchased gates to put on the entrances of the house to prevent him from leaving without a key. Out of all my friends, we were the only ones with iron gates. We called them bars because we likened the iron gates to a prison cell. These gates required a key to exit and enter the house. Therefore, anyone coming in or out had to ask our parents to unlock the door.

When I was younger, being jailed in this manner was worse than a math class at 7:20 am. Even if I wanted to go to the backyard to play basketball for an hour or two, I would have to ask my mom or dad to open the gate, which was more than irritating. On the days they said yes, if I wanted to come back in the house, we would have to knock on the door until someone answered because they couldn't keep the door unlocked. As an adult, I understand my parents took those extreme measures to protect Anderson. I am glad they did.

On the flip side, there is no doubt of negative effects to living with parents driven by fear. Debbie Rigaud, author of *Perfect Shot and Hallway Diaries*, names the following fear-based parenting mistakes: being overprotective, using no as a default response, sheltering your kids, always casting suspicion, and clinging to outdated ideals.[8] These negative behaviors are counterproductive and debilitating. On the other hand, the same fear that causes parents to behave in such a manner could ultimately help their children grow to be strong, aware, and productive adults. It is perfectly reasonable for a parent to protect their children, say no when necessary, have them explore the world, ask probing questions, and teach them good tradition all out of fear. Fear is not exclusively bad. Fear can be useful. The question is: How can you use fear to your advantage?

You have the ability to decide how you can use fear in your own life. If you decide to allow it to place manacles around your feet, you will never GO. Here are a few fears I think about a lot that bring kneejerk responses:

- I am afraid to die without leaving a legacy. But it is hard to actually leave a mark, and most people fail at doing so.
- I am afraid to be forty years old and not married. But it is hard to find a woman I actually like. There are not enough fish in the sea.
- I am afraid to retire at the age of seventy with no savings. But most people do, and the government is there to help.

- I am afraid of my community remaining in the same state for fifty years without positive change or improvement. But people are hardheaded and prefer to stick with tradition.

In all of these scenarios, I acknowledged my fears as an actual possibility, and I allowed the prospect of failure to blind me to a solution. The *actiophil*, on the other hand, would have a different response to those same fears. Here is a better way to respond:

- I am afraid to die without leaving a legacy. Therefore, I will pursue my goals with the time and energy I have now.
- I am afraid to be forty years old and not married. Therefore, I have to be courageous in speaking with women who pique my interest.
- I am afraid to retire at the age of seventy with no savings. Therefore, I will seek residual streams of income and make wise retirement strategies.
- I am afraid of my community remaining in the same state for fifty years without positive change or improvement. Therefore, I will create opportunities in my community to help foster advancement and mentor the downtrodden.

Same fears, different attitudes. In the first scenarios, I decided to use fear as the exact reason why I should not cross the starting line. In the second scenario, I used fear to elevate my desire for a positive outcome. If you want to break past the wall and cross the starting line, you must transfer your fear into a success-driven engine. Your attitude about fear will determine the likelihood of that fear becoming a reality.

Put Fear Behind You

One day when I was young, my sister and I were playing outside. As we careened around the house, we encountered our neighbor on the other side of the fence holding a golden-brown puppy named Chi Chi with charming eyes. We were delighted to see the puppy because our parents were categorically opposed to having pets. With baited breathe, we asked our neighbor to let us hold the puppy. He said yes. My sister held the puppy first while we both petted her... until I asked to hold Chi Chi. Ten seconds after I received the wriggling mass of fur, she slipped from my hand and fell hard on the ground. At that moment, I believed that Chi Chi hated me with the anger of a thousand dragons.

Once Chi Chi grew sharp teeth and was old enough to run, she would chase me to the ends of the earth. Whenever I exited my house during my teenage years, I would literally (and I mean literally) fear for my life. I never walked outside without knowing exactly where Chi Chi was and what she was doing. Especially in the mornings when I had to walk to the bus stop to head to school. Thankfully, most mornings, she was locked in the neighbor's house. But on the off days, we would either have to sneak to the other side of the street and tiptoe silently by or circle completely around the next block, adding fifteen minutes to our route. Due to my ninja-like techniques, I was only chased by Chi Chi approximately ten times. On those times, I ran like Usain Bolt being chased by a Cheetah! *I have come to realize, whenever Chi Chi is chasing me, I never run backward. I always run forward.*

> *You have the decision to make fear your focal point or place positive outcomes in your line of vision.*

Unless you are transferring fear to be used for good, it should be behind you. If you allow fear to get in front of you, it will either cause you to stop or run backward. The question is: How can you put fear behind you?

Once again, it is a decision. You must choose to focus on positive outcomes as opposed to negative results. Margie Warrell, Forbes contributing writer and a global authority on brave leadership, wrote, "When we put our attention on things that create anxiety and fear, it only triggers past memories of other events that made us feel anxious and afraid…keep you focus on those things that create the positive empowering emotions that will keep your head in the right place and direct your actions for optimal outcomes."[9] Stephen Covey, author of the international best-selling book *7 Habits of Highly Effective People*, encourages his readers to "Begin with the end in mind."[10] He writes, "All things are created twice. There is a mental or first creation, and a physical or second creation to all things. The physical creation follows the mental, just as a building follows a blueprint. If you don't make a conscious effort to visualize who you are and what you want in life, then you empower other people and circumstances to shape you and your life by default."[11]

You have the decision to make fear your focal point or place positive outcomes in your line of vision. You can choose to run toward anxiety or let fear chase you. The finish line can be your driving force or fear can steer you toward dead ends. If you desire to cross the starting line, a decision has to be made. Not tomorrow. Today! The reason I had perfect attendance almost every year in middle and high school was because my focus was on getting to school, not on Chi Chi. If I had decided to base all my decisions on whether or not the dog was outside, I would never have made it past our front door. Instead, I acknowledged the potential of being chased while concluding my education was more important than my fear. I decided to run toward school, not back into the house.

Create Courage, Abandon Anxiety

Fear is rational.

Let me explain. I understand why people are afraid. We know death is always at our doorstep. Statistically, there is a high chance your business will not stand the test of time. Shikhar Ghosh, a senior lecturer at the Harvard Business School, reported, "75 percent of venture-backed companies never return cash to investors, with 30 to 40 percent of those liquidating assets where investors lose all of their money."[12] McKinley Irvin Family Law published, "In America, there is one divorce approximately every 36 seconds. That's nearly 2,400 divorces per day, 16,800 divorces per week and 876,000 divorces a year."[13] Slate stated that the United States has "the lowest college completion rate in the developed world."[14] These are facts. Given such facts, it makes sense to approach the starting line with caution and trepidation.

However, negative statistics are not the authors of your life story. I repeat. **Negative statistics are not the authors of your life story.** In the face of a gloomy outcome, your goal should be to create courage, not abandon anxiety. Preparing yourself for success gives you more opportunity than bracing for failure.

In middle school, I was a scrawny, funny-lookin', shoes-too-large-for-my-feet type of kid. A friend of mine (whom I consider a brother), David Doirin, use to take me to his wrestling practices at North Miami Beach Senior High (NMB), a local high school. While these wrestlers trained in the weight room, I always admired their work ethic and strength. They would measure their toughness by how much they could bench press. The standard was two plates, which equaled 225 pounds—the bar weighed 45 pounds, plus two 45-pound weights on both sides of the bar. At that age, I was never able to lift that weight. When I made it to high school and enrolled in the Weight Training class, my goal was to lift two plates off my chest.

At the first opportunity, I attempted two plates, but I was unable to lift the bar off the rack. Then my spotter removed 90 pounds. Still nothing. By this time, everyone was looking at me in amazement at how weak I was. In disbelief, they removed all the plates to see if I could even lift the bar (45 pounds), which was the absolute lowest amount of weight someone can bench press. I remember using all the strength in my body to lift the bar off the rack, bringing it down to my chest, and almost forcing the soul out my body to clear my chest. But to my dismay and the enjoyment of everyone in the weight room, I was unable to do so. As people ran to help me with amusement, the weight room erupted in laughter at my muscular deficiency. At that point, I wished my soul had left my body.

    I had a choice to make. I could decide never to attempt lifting the bar again, or I could train myself to get stronger and eventually succeed. I chose the second option. Over the next couple of weeks, I began doing pushups religiously to get stronger in my chest and triceps. Day after day, I exercised those muscles to prepare me for Take 2. Eventually, I felt ready to get back on the bench. I called on everything within me to lift the bar off the rack, bring it down to my chest, and push as though I was giving birth! Through the struggle and pain, I eventually managed to make it to the finish line, and everyone cheered. Instead of focusing on my fear of embarrassment, I did what I could to get better.

Dear *actiophil*, if you want to cross the starting line, you must get stronger at what you can do. I figured I couldn't lift the bar, but I could do pushups. I dedicated my time to strengthen the areas directly around my weakness. Here is the trick: *replace worry with work*. When you do that, you become more brave and courageous. Instead of getting rid of fear, you can overpower fear. The negativity and possibility of failure will always be there. But it doesn't have to stop you from crossing the starting line. As President Rosenberg says, "[We do not] ask for a lighter load, but broader shoulders."[15] Decreasing your level of fear is ideal; however, strengthening your bravery gives you the optimal opportunity to overcome anxiety and fear.

Laziness

When I was a student at Valencia College in Orlando, I lived in an apartment with three other housemates at The Village of Alafaya Club. We shared the same living space, but each of us had separate rooms and bathrooms. Over the course of two years, housemates moved in and out. The last six months that I lived at the Alafaya Club, a gentleman originally from Morocco moved in from Philadelphia. His mindset, culture, and way of living were different from mine. One habit he had that I did not fully understand (and still don't to this day) was his unwillingness to use microwaves. Whenever he had to warm food, he would turn on the oven, wait for it to preheat, set the food on aluminum foil, place it in the heated oven, and wait a long time until the food was warm. The whole process took approximately forty-five minutes. When I needed warm food, it would take a mere forty-five seconds via the microwave.

In this age of the microwave, I find it inconceivable to wait over thirty minutes to warm up my food. It suffices to say, when it comes to food, I literally have a microwave mentality. A sad reality I have come to notice is that many people carry that mindset beyond the parameters of food. "Faster Faster Faster" has become the mantra for any and everything. We want to drive faster, lose weight faster, get a job faster, graduate faster, get into relationships faster, and get our food faster. However, "Faster Faster Faster" does not equate to "Better Better Better." *Our deep desire to receive everything now kills our willingness to strive for goals that may come tomorrow.*

Now, here is the paradox: this book is predicated entirely on the fact that you need to cross the starting line. I want you to GO! However, I have just expressed discontent regarding being too hasty. Here is why: action does not always equal productivity. As the ten-time NCAA championship coach John Wooden says, "Never mistake activity for achievement."[16] On the other hand, stagnancy gives you zero chance of productivity. Laziness is a silent disease that suffocates more dreams than impulsive behavior.

Nando Pelusi, PhD, member of the National Association of Cognitive-Behavioral Therapists advisory board wrote, "Accomplishing practically anything today means overcoming the need for instant gratification."[17] Pelusi also penned, "Once we've generated a goal, we believe that we've got to do something about it. We're torn between competing desires: I want to accomplish this idealized plan, but it must not be too hard. In fact, I need it to be easy."[18] To express these words in plain English: We want to reach the finish line only if the journey is short and simple. This impatience to reach our desired outcome produces laziness. If the finish line does not immediately follow the starting line, most people will not bother to GO. Folks would prefer to procrastinate until they feel the finish line is as close to the starting line as possible. In turn, this procrastination results in outright laziness.

Thankfully, there is a cure for the disease of laziness. The solution is found in patience. As the old saying goes, "Rome was not built in one day." Greatness takes time. While our insistence on cutting corners is produced by laziness, it is important to distinguish between not moving forward because of sloth and not starting as a strategy.

Process Merges Purpose and Patience

Crossing the starting line is less about looking productive and more about producing purposeful outcomes. My intent for this book is not to encourage you to start because it looks or feels good; I want you to have a motivating factor that underpins all the decisions you make. Do not cross the starting line because everyone else is doing it. You need a genuine reason that erupts from the inside and causes you to take action. Unless you have a purpose for starting, stay patient.

While being patient, put yourself through a process to be equipped for the journey after you start. Jon Mertz, one of the Top 100 Thought Leaders in Trustworthy Business wrote, "We need to embrace our life and what it can mean, what it should mean, and what we are meant for it to mean. When we get our process of life right, we get our purpose right. And when we get our purpose right, our process of doing the work enables our purpose to come to life."[19]

Process separates lazy waiting from patience. In the spirit of crossing the starting line, let's take Usain Bolt for example. He is an Olympian from Jamaica who holds the world record and gold medal in the 100 meters, 200 meters and 4 × 100 meters relay. When I think of running a race, I only think of going as fast as I can. But when runners think of a race, they think of a strategy, running methods, and process.

World-renowned sports scientist, Dr. Nicholas Romanov, analyzed Usain Bolt's running technique, saying, "In my understanding, the most important factor is that Bolt uses gravity, to be more exact, gravitational torque, as the leading factor that allows him to more effectively involve all other forces, working as a whole and highly effective system for horizontal repositioning of the athlete with high velocity. Simply speaking, in his running he uses rotation of the body around the point of support under the action of gravitational torque, which in essence is a free falling of the body forward."[20]

Reading this shocked me. Running a race is more than going fast. It's also understanding how to go fast. If Usain Bolt had not gone through the process of learning how to optimize his speed, he probably would not have qualified to run in the Olympics for Jamaica. But the process takes patience. The first time Usain Bolt crossed the starting line to represent Jamaica as an Olympian was in 2004 at Athens. But he was determined to compete long before then. In his younger years, he actually enjoyed playing cricket more than running. But his father saw how fast he ran and suggested he run track. According to *The Guardian*, Usain Bolt's father told him to "do running because it's an individual sport, and if you do good, you do good for yourself."[21]

That purpose merged with the process, which led to patience. People downplayed Usain Bolt's greatness. He suffered from a condition called Scoliosis, which caused a curvature in his spine, causing one of his legs to be shorter than another by half an inch. All of those setbacks could have caused him to retreat to laziness. But instead, he remained patient and crossed the starting line to eventually win multiple gold medals, break speed records, and become the fastest person in the world.

Depending on a person's end goal, the purpose must be married with the process, which produces patience that kills laziness. As alluded to earlier, laziness is not synonymous with patience. Part of the distinct difference between the two comes from the reason for standing still. As an *actiophil*, you can only be described as patient (and not lazy) if you stall with a purpose.

Work While You Wait

From an outside perspective, it is difficult to determine if someone is being lazy or patient. In reality, there is a sharp distinction between the two. For example, say I set a goal to begin weight training in order to build ten pounds of muscle in three months, and I tell a couple of friends about my goal. If one month later they check on my progress and learn I haven't started my gym membership, they may think I am being lazy. That would be understandable. But what if the only gym near my house was under renovation? In that case, I was being patient for the gym to reopen. My friends would have to reconsider whether or not I was lazy.

Oxford Dictionary defines patience as "the capacity to accept or tolerate delay, problems, or suffering without becoming annoyed or anxious."[22] Lazy is defined as "unwilling to work or use energy."[23] Those two definitions tell different stories, similar to the likely changed perspective of my friends once they understood the reason I did not start the gym membership.

For an *actiophil*, being patient is not an excuse for doing nothing. Waiting for the right conditions in order to optimize success is not the same as waiting for an opportunity to come knocking. In the previous scenario, although I couldn't sign up for the gym membership, that did not prevent me from working out at my house. I could have begun my muscle building by doing pushups, pull ups, or chin ups; I did not need a gym membership to do any of those things.

There is always an alternative to doing nothing. If the ideal scenario for crossing the starting line is unavailable, you must proactively seek the best alternative. Don't wait around. *Lucky breaks are not available to those who rely on luck.*

An old saying goes, "When opportunity comes knocking, will you be ready?" However, I contend that opportunity is rarely knocking on doors. *Opportunity does not exist for those unready to receive it.* Opportunity is not something you can wait on. Opportunity is a place you arrive at once you are ready. If you desire to become an attorney, no matter how many law firms are looking to hire new attorneys, that opportunity is not available to you if you did not go to law school and pass the bar exam. Period! Your desire to practice law means nothing if it is not coupled with action. Laziness is a disease that surfaces with the guise of patience. The cure is to work while you wait. Work on educating yourself about the details of what you are about to start. Work on building relationships with those in the field you want to cross into. Work on identifying skills you need to strengthen your chances of success on the journey. Work on yourself.

Start with your Neighborhood

If you ask any ambitious person, "What would you like to do in the future?" a common response is, "I would like to change the world." Grant Cardone, author of *The 10x Rule: The Only Difference Between Success and Failure*, wrote about the importance of setting goals ten times greater than your belief in attaining those goals. Cardone shared the importance of stretching yourself beyond your perceived limits, stating that you will go much farther if you aim beyond what you believe is possible. I support the "shoot for the stars" mindset and urge all *actiophils* to never settle for good or great and instead aim for remarkable.

Although I encourage the finish line to be glamorous, shining, and extraordinary, the starting line does not need that same splendor. Because of a false sense of responsibility, many people do not start the journey. They get intimidated by the idea of changing the world. The burden of changing culture, influencing laws, or building an international coalition can indeed be stressful and intimidating. When you stand in front of a mountain of obligation, it is understandable why you would feel small and why that feeling of inadequacy would lead to a default action of doing nothing. This, in turn, leads to laziness.

The solution should not be buckle up and drive hopelessly into a tornado of unlimited tasks. Instead, the first aim should be to start with your neighborhood. Doing so is more realistic and manageable. The neighborhood can be your training ground for the world.

Let's take Rosa Parks as an example. We know her today as the civil rights activist who refused to surrender her seat to a white passenger on a segregated bus in Montgomery, Alabama. This led to, according to Biography.com, the Montgomery Bus Boycott, which spearheaded a nationwide effort to end the racial segregation of public facilities. Many years later, Rosa Parks received the Presidential Medal of Freedom, the highest honor given by the United States' executive branch. The next year, she was awarded the Congressional Gold Medal, the highest award given by the US legislative branch.[24]

But Rosa Parks did not begin as a nationally acclaimed civil rights powerhouse. Rather, she crossed the starting line by joining the Montgomery chapter of the NAACP in 1943, serving as the chapter's youth leader. Rosa Parks started with her neighborhood. She was a local change maker before becoming a national icon. Dear *actiophil*, do not allow the weight of your end goal to press you down into a chair of complacency. Every big finish has a small beginning.

Delusion of Perfection

Bobby Hoffman, PhD, author of *Motivation for Learning and Performance*, penned, "The odds of being dealt the perfect hand in poker (royal straight flush) happens on average every 649,739 hands. In baseball, a perfect game (no base-runners allowed) occurs once every 18,192 games. In bowling, an adult male will need approximately 11,500 opportunities to attain a perfect score (300)."[25] In poker, baseball, and bowling, perfection is not impossible, but it is rare enough to not be expected. Many people do not cross the starting line because they are obsessed with being perfect.

I too struggled with the idea of perfection. For most of my life, I carried the false notion that perfection is attainable. On many occasions, I entered hours-long debates on the feasibility of living an error-free life. If you had asked me back then if I won those debates, my answer would probably have been, "Of course I won! It would have been impossible to make a better argument." Fast forwarding to today, if you ask me if perfection is achievable, my answer would be one two-letter word: no. Thankfully, I ditched those false thoughts before my first book. Or else I would never have crossed the starting line to publish.

> Excellence is the human version of perfection.

My first book, *Powerful Presenting: How to Overcome One of the Greatest Fears*, was far from perfect. While working on the first draft, I agonized over minor details. For every sentence I wrote, it took me an extra ten minutes to analyze the sentence structure to ensure the words were perfect. When I was finally done with the manuscript, I sent it to someone to edit. To my surprise, she found a myriad of errors. It was as if I had typed the book with my eyes closed. She edited everything. I was wholly satisfied after rereading it. Then I had someone else look at the edited version. They were flabbergasted at the sheer number of errors and poor sentence structure. My jaw dropped in shock as well. We then proceeded to spend more time editing the book than it had taken to write it. Upon completion of that process, we said, "Enough is enough; it is time to publish." Thankfully we did. Within a year, the book reached close to a thousand readers.

People loved it! But guess what? To this day, we continue to discover mistakes that we never caught before.

If I had waited to be perfect, I would never have published a book at the age of twenty-three. Nor would I have applied for graduate school or run for student body president at the university. I did those things despite my flaws. To my joy, I succeeded in those endeavors. I overcame the false notion of perfection, and so can you.

The delusion of perfection has many causes. Some are self-evident, while others are hidden. I discovered that excellence is the human version of perfection. The consequences of having a Delusion of Perfection will lead to The Imposter Syndrome and Visionary Paralysis. If you are impaired by a delusion of perfection, regardless of why, it's necessary to overcome the delusion. Let's discuss Imposter Syndrome and Visionary Paralysis.

The Imposter Syndrome

In November 2018, the Princeton and Harvard law graduate, lawyer, and former First Lady of the United States, Michelle Obama, released her most recent book titled *Becoming*. While on a book tour at an all-girls high school in North London, Michelle Obama shared insight into her life that shocked the world. She stated, "I still have a little [bit of] impostor syndrome, it never goes away, that you're actually listening to me. It never goes away, that feeling that you shouldn't take me that seriously. What do I know?"[26] This statement was surprising given her level of accomplishments and the high esteem in which society holds her.

But thankfully her statement did not end there. She continued: "I share that with you because we all have doubts in our abilities, about our power and what that power is…Here is the secret. I have been at probably every powerful table that you can think of, I have worked at nonprofits, I have been at foundations, I have worked in corporations, served on corporate boards, I have been at G-summits, I have sat in at the UN; they are not that smart."[27]

You may feel like an imposter because you think people expect you to be perfect. You may feel like an imposter because you are keenly aware of your deep flaws. You may feel like an imposter because people constantly devalue your voice. You may feel like an imposter because society abandoned you. You may feel like an imposter because you believed that your entire life and don't know why.

Dear *actiophil*, you are not an imposter! The words of Michelle Obama—"they are not that smart"—sent shock waves around the world. She exposed the lie that society tells you and me. We do not need a halo of perfection to get started. Diligence is what is required. The only people who are truly imposters are those who lied and cheated their way to the finish line. If you do not fit that description, do not worry.

You can never be an imposter in your own dream. You are the best person available to write the script for your life. The songwriter and producer Swoope eloquently said, "Perfection is the goal but excellence is accepted."[28] The Hall of Fame NFL coach Vince Lombardi said, "Perfection is not attainable, but if we chase perfection we can catch excellence."[29] Perfection is available to no person. Conditions will never be perfect to cross the starting line. Stop waiting. GO!

Visionary Paralysis

I remember watching a video in 2015 by Eric Thomas (ET) that electrified me. He said, "What you cannot do is quit during the process. It's when you have nothing left, it's when you depleted all your money, when all your energy's gone, when you have nothing left...that's when it's Showtime. When you find a way out of no way, when you find breath that you didn't have before, when you find energy that did not exist, when you want this thing as bad as you want to breathe...that's when you find a way."[30] I got pumped up! Immediately, I sped to Walmart and purchased large sheets of arts and crafts paper. On one sheet, I wrote my vision for the future. On the other sheet, I wrote why I would accomplish that vision. Then I taped those large sheets to the wall. Above those sheets, I wrote on a piece of printing paper, "My dreams are too large to stay in my head."

With this newfound dedication, my mind began exploring at rapid paces different ideas I could execute to reach the goals I had set out for myself. I was writing everything down so that when my mind relaxed, I could go through everything and choose the best possible path to take. *This is great!* I thought to myself. I was developing a full-proof plan to retire my parents, begin investments that my future children could benefit from, and ways my surrounding community could grow as a result. As I reached the entrepreneurial climax of ideas, I began to have what I call visionary paralysis. In a video I made in tribute to Eric Thomas, I introduced the term. It simply means "the ability of the mind to match your extraordinary vision with extraordinary doubts." Here are some of the transcripts from my video:

> *The same ability that you have to come up with something creative and innovative to make change, is the same ability that you have to come up with negative thoughts to hinder that change. That is what I call visionary paralysis. While we see the mountaintop, we see the top of Mount Everest, and we have a plan on how to get there. We become confused and hindered by little hills...if you spend the entire time tripping over hills saying, "Ah there's a speed bump, I can't start today. I can't start this year...ah look at that speed bump, ahh man, it's hindering me, the world is aga—" NO! the world is not against you. You are against you. My friends, at one point, I had visionary paralysis. I would come up with extraordinary ideas but then come up with extraordinarily negative thoughts...*[31]

Visionary paralysis crippled me in the past because I was deluded by visions of a perfect outcome. Imagine what the world would be like if the Wright brothers had allowed negative thoughts to cloud their desire to see a man fly. They had every reason to quit and lead regular lives. But they didn't.

How would the transportation industry look if Henry Ford had decided to follow convention and settle for the ordinary? Elon Musk could have lived comfortably off the money he made from selling PayPal, but he decided to start Space X and Tesla, both of which are now valued over a billion dollars. What would the state of America be if a "skinny kid" from Chicago had not pursued his dream of being president despite never having witness a person of his skin color who sat in the highest office? Barack Obama could have declared his term as senator of Chicago the zenith of his life, and rightfully so. But Obama yearned for more and eventually became the nation's first black president despite fierce opposition.

The Wright Brothers, Ford, Musk, and Obama are individuals who did not allow visionary paralysis to chain them to comfort; they crossed the starting line despite convention arguing against their chosen paths.

Cures to Visionary Paralysis

1) Yes, We Can Philosophy

Obama did not get elected into the Oval Office because of "Yes I Can" but because of "Yes We Can." Obama understood that in spite of all of his might and intelligence, he was able to take himself only so far—not far enough to reach his destiny. Therefore, he actively sought out the real needs of "everyday people" and built a platform around addressing those needs. Obama did not capitulate to the self-serving interest of "the few" but decided to speak on behalf of the "many." If Obama's mentality had been "Yes I can," his name would not have rung bells past the city limits of Chicago.

Please understand that you do not need "many" people to get started. However, if you are the only one benefiting from what you are trying to accomplish while others are being negatively affected, your plan or project will die a thousand deaths after you cross the starting line. People are important. Always keep others in mind regardless if you need them or not. There are always good or bad consequences for everything you do. Thus, key to overcoming visionary paralysis is residing in the mindset of "Yes We Can."

2) Snap Out the Vision, Step Into Reality

In *Powerful Presenting*, I spoke about visualizing success. To the surprise of many readers, I did not echo the same, trite message that most motivational speakers repeat. Although I advocate for the need to visualize the finish line, research suggests too much visualization can yield negative consequences. Researchers Heather Barry Kappes and Gabriele Oettingen found that "positive fantasies predict poor achievement because they do not generate energy to pursue the desired future."[32]

The idea of a better future is so desirable that many people spend their lives thinking about it. The vision of the finish line is so sweet that people would rather bask in that feeling than take a step toward that reality. The longer you stay in front of the starting line, the more visionary paralysis will affect you. Stop imagining a better future. *GO* into it.

3) Cross, Cross, and Cross Again

On November 24, 1888, a young boy was born on an obscure farm in Maryville, Missouri.[33] This child was raised under deplorable conditions. In his early years, he woke up at four in the morning every day to milk the cows on the farm. Poverty was so rampant one would have thought their family was cursed. Although this young man was dealt an extremely bad hand in life, he committed to making something of himself. He eventually went to college, graduated, and began selling correspondence courses to ranchers. From there, he went on to sell bacon, soap, and lard for Armour & Company. Given his upbringing, he could have settled with that taste of success and raised his hands to the heavens in thanksgiving for leading a better life than his parents.

> *If you are the only one benefiting from what you are trying to accomplish while others are being negatively affected, your plan or project will die a thousand deaths after you cross the starting line.*

But this young boy wanted more. He eventually quit his job to pursue his dream of becoming a Chautauqua lecturer.

But he had no luck in that endeavor. So then he chased a career in acting but found little success there. Here was a young man from Missouri who had been raised in desperate poverty now an adult in New York living in unspeakable conditions. But this young lad had a lot of fight left. He began teaching public speaking courses at the local YMCA night school, and it was soon evident that he had found his niche. He became a sought-after teacher and eventually developed a course that brought in a lot of money and helped many people. From there, he decided to write a book titled *Art of Public Speaking*. As you can imagine, the book did not sell too well. But that did not stop him. He went on to write four more books:

1. Public Speaking: The Standard Course of the United Y. M. C. A. Schools (1920)
2. Public Speaking: A Practical Course for Business Men (1926)
3. Lincoln, the Unknown (1932)
4. Little Known Facts about Well Known People (1934)

Once again, he experienced discouraging results. At that point in his life, he could have sat back and continued with his speaking courses and made some royalties from his previous five books. But he believed he had at least one more book in him. As fate had it, he did.

This gentlemen, Dale Carnegie, wrote the book *How to Win Friends and Influence People*. It was an immediate hit. Before he died, the book was translated in over twenty languages, sold over five million copies, and still sells close to two hundred thousand copies per year.

When he first released the book, Dale Carnegie did not have a clue how powerful and effective it was. But it eventually made him a superstar of presidential proportions. Dale became one of the most famous people in the country. If *Little Known Facts about Well Known People* had been his last writing effort, no one today would know who he was. But because of his resolve to continuously cross the starting line, we now know Dale Carnegie as the father of personal development.

Dear *actiophil*, simply because you cross the starting line once does not mean you will reach the finish line. It may take two tries or twenty. Do not break, bend, or be discouraged. Your determination will bring forth your destiny. If a skinny boy with big ears born to a poor family in Missouri can become one of the best-selling authors of all time, you can go to law school. Or learn a new language. Or pass the treacherous math class. Or maybe even move out of the country. Whatever the starting line is, you can cross it! Each time you cross the starting line, you shatter visionary paralysis. GO!

Unhealthy Relationships

Having strong relationships is a matter of life and death. Literally. Jane E Brody, in a *New York Times* article titled *Social Interaction is Critical for Mental and Physical Health*, shared a myriad of research studies pointing to the necessity of healthy relationships. Reading through these studies, I was shocked by the impact of our relationships on our health. One report Brody shared from, the *Harvard Women's Health Watch* stated, "People who have satisfying relationships with family, friends and their community are happier, have fewer health problems, and live longer."[34] An article published by Forbes titled *Research Shows Bad Relationships can Also Mean Bad Health* reported, "Constant tension or serious conflicts in a relationship can keep your body in flight-or-flight mode all the time, spurring your body to produce adrenaline and quickly discard the excess. This can eventually lead to fatigue, a weakened immune system, and even organ damage."[35]

In addition to the aforementioned consequences of bad relationships, being part of the wrong crowd can also lead a person to stress, depression, anxiety, and feelings of low self-esteem. Given the negative effects unhealthy relationships have on mental and physical health, it makes sense why many people do not cross the starting line. The relationships you are in— whether intimate, platonic, or familial—impact your will to GO. In an earlier section regarding fear, I shared that my goal for you is that you not only abandon anxiety but also create courage. Similarly, my goal in this section is to encourage strong relationships. This will help you shed the unhealthy relationships in your life that are hindering you from crossing the starting line.

> When I look back at all the positive changes in my life, I can see the fingerprints of my friends and family all over my victories.

One of my best friends, Brandon Benjamin, is one of the most intelligent people I know. The first time I met him, we were sophomores in high school. At first, Brandon was a mystery to everyone. He hadn't attended the school as a freshman, and as a sophomore, he started off the year relatively quiet. As the weeks and months progressed, however, he began speaking often and showing more of himself. It turned out that Brandon was extremely funny. On a daily basis, he and I had the classroom laughing at every and any joke, much to the chagrin of our teacher. Brandon and I grew to become great friends, and eventually I was the best man in his wedding.

As I mentioned earlier, I was never a great student; my grades dragged along from semester to semester, while Brandon's grades hovered around As and sometimes Bs. I admired his knowledge, diction, and ability to retain information. When I began developing a thirst for education, he was the first person I attached myself to. Every day, I would call or text him to speak about a new concept I had learned or a new word I had come across, or to figure out what he was teaching himself. We would send each other videos of Ted Talks, philosophers, or someone being bombastic. As a result of my strong relationship with Brandon, my vocabulary shot through the roof. My ability to receive and retain knowledge increased dramatically. I became a better person.

Had it not been for Brandon, I would not have the capacity to write this book. Our relationship created a domino effect that is still knocking down walls of fear and failure to this day. I have become a better person because I surround myself with people who are better than me. When I look back at all the positive changes in my life, I can see the fingerprints of my friends and family all over my victories. Here are a few examples:

- My father, Ramces Noel: integrity and character helped raise me to become a strong man
- My mother, Marie Lafalaise-Noel: authenticity and love helped me to see the beauty in others
- My older brother, David Noel: diligence and grit encourages me to ALWAYS plan to succeed, then execute
- My sister, Makisha Noel: audacity to always believe and fearlessness taught me to live without constraints
- My younger brother, Anderson Noel: warmth and appreciation for life teaches me to focus on the important things in life

These are only my immediate family members. This book would be far too long if I attempted to name everyone who contributed to my success. Healthy relationships are part of the reason I can cross the starting line without looking back. My question to you is: Why haven't you crossed the starting line yet?

In the same way that I am determined to attach myself to positive influences, I am equally steadfast in avoiding negative friendships. Bad company has the power to drain positive energy. Kim Staudenraus, founder of "Striving…To Do Life Better," told the story of a Pastor who demonstrated this concept perfectly:

> *Several years ago at church the pastor had an example on stage where he stood on a chair and asked one of the*

elders to stand in front of him on the floor. The pastor then attempted to pull the elder up onto the chair. He wrapped his arms around the elder, under his arms and pulled up. The pastor struggled and strained but as much as he tried with all his body weight and strength he could not pull the elder up onto the chair.

Then the pastor asked the elder to attempt to pull him down off the chair. The elder grabbed a hold of the pastor's hand and with one quick pull and step forward the pastor came down off the chair. The elder used hardly any energy what-so-ever.[36]

There are people in your life right now who are cancerous to your success. They are blood-sucking leeches that exhaust your energy, squander your time, and poke holes in your wallet. These people can be your parents, siblings, cousins, friends, or colleagues. But interestingly enough, they are rarely your enemies. I have learned quickly in life that my failures are rarely a result of adversary but connected instead to people I have trusted. Someone can only pull you down if you lend them your hand. But the interesting part is, you will never lend your hand to someone you know hates you.

Dear *actiophil*, in order to cross the starting line, you need support. I repeat: YOU NEED SUPPORT! Here is how to abandon unhealthy relationships and run toward the finish line:

The Diamond Dynamic

Diamonds are expensive; ask any man looking to purchase a 1-carat diamond ring to propose to his girlfriend. Those price tags sport a lot of digits. A carat is a unit of weight for precious stones and pearls. According to Zoara, "The average person will spend around $6,000 on a 1-carat diamond for an engagement ring. This may seem like a lot, but 1-carat diamonds can actually fetch over $25,000, depending on their characteristics and quality."[37] For the sake of example, let's examine the average price of a carat at $6,000. A carat equals 0.000440925 of a pound. This means 1 pound would equal approximately 2268 carats. Therefore, a one-pound diamond would cost approximately $1,360,800. I repeat: a one-pound diamond would cost ONE MILLION, THREE HUNDRED SIXTY THOUSAND, EIGHT HUNDRED DOLLARS! I won't even calculate how much a one-pound diamond would cost if you are purchasing one carat for $25,000. You can do the math.

Dear *actiophil*, diamonds are expensive. But there is a price that is higher than a one-pound diamond. That price is your purpose. Competent people of goodwill wearing orange jumpsuits are locked away in cages as a result to poor friendships. Every day, we drive past people wearing expensive suits who are six feet underground because their connections with the wrong crowd. Many folks are afraid to live their dreams and instead choose to live their nightmare because of their circle of friends. I know people who want to travel the world but instead elect to chain themselves within a three-mile radius of their neighborhood because of their companions. If you want to cross the starting line, you need a Dynamic Diamond of friends (see figure 2)—at least one mentor, two compeers, and one mentee. Let's start with compeer.

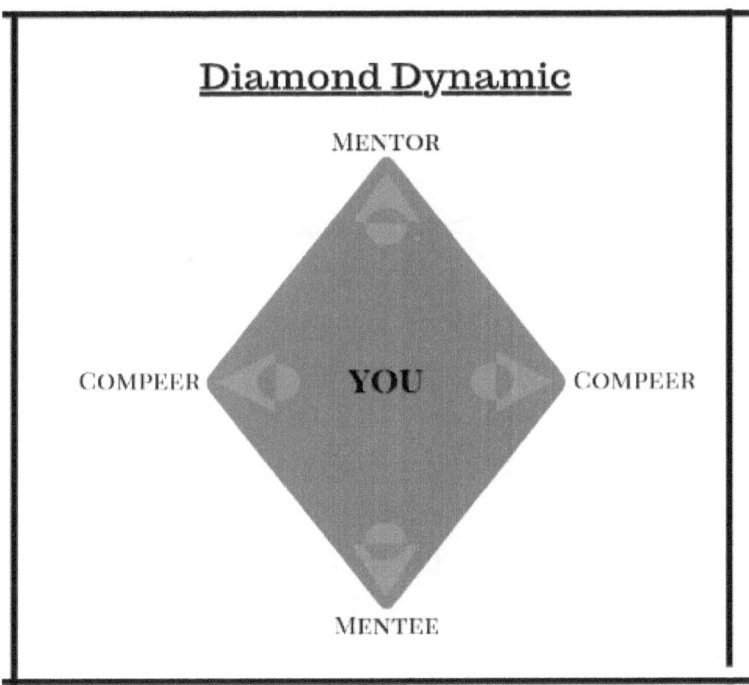

Figure 2

Compeer:

When you saw the phrase Dynamic Diamond, probably the first question you asked is why I chose two compeers as opposed to two friends. First, let's define compeer. *Oxford Dictionary* describes compeer as "a person of equal rank, status, or ability."[38] This differs from how we commonly describe friendship. For example, I have friends who are studying to take the Law School Admission Test (LSAT) before applying to Law School. Although we are friends, I am unfit to help them study or prepare for the test; practicing law never interested me, plus I don't have enough working knowledge on the subject. It would be unwise of them to cross the starting line with me. I'm a friend, not a compeer.

Here is another example: Students in highly technical fields such as law, medicine, and engineering are more inclined to form study groups among those in their class. My sophomore year at Valencia College, I roomed with Raul, a senior studying civil engineering at the University of Central Florida. When Raul attempted to teach me what he was learning in class, I thought he was speaking another language. I did not understand why one problem would take more than three pages to solve. But when his engineering classmates came over, they all spoke that same language! Although I was Raul's friend, I was in no position to help. I was nowhere near "equal rank, status, or ability."

As I was writing my first book, a friend of mine, David Frederick, was also writing a book. We shot the breeze many a day about writing strategy, our progress, our difficulties, and the challenge of finding harmony between completing the book and not losing focus on our everyday life. David's support as my "running" companion gave me the fortitude to cross the finish line. The similarity of our struggles and concerns helped me not feel lonely during the book-writing or publishing process. David Frederick was determined to cross the starting line, and that determination helped me do the same. He was my compeer.

Ask yourself this question: Are the people by your side wavering between a yellow and green light, or are they determined to GO? If they are not determined to start, they are not compeers. My compeers gifted me with two great blessings:

1. I had someone to grow with.
2. I was able to easily measure my success on the journey.

Find one or two compeers and stick with them along the journey.

Mentor:

In seventh and eighth grade, I attended North Dade Middle School, which required students to wear uniforms. I preferred it that way because uniforms eliminated the expense of purchasing new clothes. Over time, I began noticing that some students came to class every Wednesday with a white buttoned-up shirt, a red tie, and black slacks. Curiosity got the best of me and I began asking around about the out-of-uniform dress on Wednesdays. Eventually I discovered these students were a part of the "5000 Role Models of Excellence Project." This program was founded by then Miami-Dade

County school board member, Frederica S. Wilson, who now serves in the United States Congress.

Congresswoman Wilson's vision for the 5000 Role Models was: "Each minority male student will graduate from high school, go to college, vocational school or the military and be positioned to become a contributing and self-sustaining member of society."[39] The goals for accomplishing that vision were:

1. *Goal #1: Place at-risk boys in supportive relationships with positive and successful men in the community who they can emulate.*
2. *Goal #2: Systematically educate program participants about the consequences of succumbing to societal pitfalls and expose them to positive alternatives to self-destructive behaviors.*
3. *Goal #3: Provide a program infrastructure that will empower adult community Role Models to assume responsibility for preparing young men to effectively deal with the challenges and struggles that threaten their success.*[40]

Upon learning of the 5000 Role Model's purpose, I begged my parents for permission to join. They gladly said yes. In my eighth grade year, I took the new member's pledge. The leaders immediately put me in touch with a mentor who would guide me and help me navigate through middle school. We visited prisons, attended events in the community, and also met professionals who gave us guidance and career advice. In high school, I joined the program again because of the value I received the first time. This proved to be a wise decision. The 5000 Role Models program continued to connect me with mentors. We went on college tours, and they took me to Tallahassee for the first time to meet congressional leaders. Upon high school graduation, the mentors gave me the tools to cross the starting line to attend college.

> *Mentoring people is one of the most selfless, yet personally empowering acts you can do.*

In college, I ensured that I would continue to have strong mentors around me for different areas of my life. Completing my master's degree would not be possible without guidance from people who were investing continuously in me. Anthony DeSantis, Assistant Vice President of Student Affairs at FIU, was one of my best resources when I needed help, advice, or connections as president of the Student Government. He also guided me through financial and academic turmoil. His coaching literally steered me out of pending failure. Crossing the starting line without a mentor is like going outside without an umbrella while it is raining. You can easily do it, but it would not be wise.

Mentee:

My sister, Makisha Noël, is a beacon of hope and strength for many people. She ignites an ever-glowing flame in the soul of everyone she encounters. And she earned every positive aspect of her life: Makisha graduated from the University of Central Florida as an entrepreneur and influencer. She has traveled the world, taking trips to Haiti, Guatemala, Peru, France, Spain, Greece, and Botswana. The trip that impacted me the most was her voyage to Istanbul, Turkey; she was sent as a United States community leader to coach Middle Eastern and North African millennials on community building and development. Given my proximity to her, I can feel her inspiration as I feel the sun on my skin.

Although Makisha has an extremely long list of accomplishments, she is most proud of having mentees, people who look up to her for guidance and support. About them, she says, "Having mentees gave me no choice but to be accountable for what I said I will do. They kept me on my toes. I was graced with mentees who are extremely ambitious and driven. They are naturally curious. They gave me the energy to be my best self, which allowed me to show up fully."[41]

Mentoring someone is one of the most selfless, yet personally empowering acts you can do. As Mary Church Terrell, one of the first African American women to earn a college degree, beautifully said, "And so, lifting as we climb, onward and upward we go, struggling and striving, and hoping that the buds and blossoms of our desires will burst into glorious fruition ere long."[42] There is unbelievable strength in helping others cross the starting line. When your mentees succeed, you win. Each time you help a mentee cross the starting line, this will give you more strength and tenacity to do the same.

Diamond Qualities

The power of relationships is undeniable when it comes to predicting future achievement. We are social creatures. Who we are and who we will be is inextricably tied with who we are around and who we are drawn to. My Diamond influences my behavior, way of thinking, and the direction I am heading. Paul, the Apostle, wrote in a letter to the church of Corinth, "Bad company corrupts good character."[43] For that reason, I am intentional about who occupies my time. Someone can be a New York Times best-selling author, but I would not accept them as a mentor if they attempted to teach me through unsavory methods. It would be irresponsible of me to have compeers who are emotionally toxic. The people I place around me must have Diamond Qualities.

The only exception could possibly be the mentee. Your primary job would be to influence them toward the right path. If they come to you without Diamond Qualities, part of your relationship with them should be instilling such qualities.

Below are Diamond (D.I.A.M.O.N.D.) Qualities that you should look for in compeers and mentors. This is important, because, in the reverse words of Paul the Apostle: Good company encourages good character.

Determined

Determination is the ability to keep one's enthusiasm and will to succeed regardless of the outcome. This attribute is high in value but low in abundance. The benefits of being determined compounds to deliver long-term success. While you work toward crossing the starting line, there must be people in your Diamond who respect their "yes." Why? Because yes is one of the most powerful words in the English language. Yes is a commitment to action despite struggle or unfavorable circumstances. People who retreat in the face of difficulty undermine the significance of yes and give rise to uncertainty. The world-renowned author and orator Anthony Robbins called determination "the wake-up call to the human will."

Inspirational

Kevin Hart is an amazing person. He is not only a comedian but also a business owner, entrepreneur, movie star, and more. He inspires me because of his ambition, his fearlessness in testing new waters, and his willingness to say yes to himself. However, as much as Kevin Hart motivates me to do better and be better, I find more inspiration from the people in my Diamond—people I interact with daily who impact my life on a personal level.

I have a friend named Noadia whom I've known since kindergarten. She is as supportive as a backbone. I remember the day she received an acceptance letter from Florida International University to join the master's program there. Her joy was infectious. She waved the letter like it was a flag of victory. Noadia joined a one-year program that would meet every single Saturday throughout the entire day from January to December. She would go to class on Saturdays, study and work on Sundays, and work full-time throughout the week, all while studying and completing assignments and projects at night. Watching her undergo that process inspired me to work toward my own master's degree. Now I am proud to join her in achieving that level of academic success.

Noadia inspired me to cross the starting line. That type of inspiration is instrumental in my life. I implore you to find mentors and compeers who have achieved or are working toward achieving inspirational goals.

> Adaptability is as indispensable to the actiophil as money is to the bank.

Adaptable

Getting stuck is almost inevitable when a person yearns to do something beyond the ordinary. By virtue of working to cross the starting line, you are venturing into an atmosphere that is uncommon and unknown. There will be ditches and dungeons to overcome en route to the finish line. But that comes with the territory of living a life of purpose. The author, actress, and businesswoman Germany Kent said, "Don't live the same day over and over again and call that a life. Life is about evolving mentally, spiritually, and emotionally."[44] Adapting is a necessary part of evolution.

Yuval Noah Harari, the best-selling author of *21 Lessons for the 21st Century* said in a Talk at Google, "Nobody knows how the world will look like in 2050. Except that it will be very different than today. So the most important thing to emphasize in education is emotional intelligence and mental stability. Because the one thing they will need for sure is the ability to reinvent themselves repeatedly."[45] The reinvention of oneself is adaption to an ever-changing social environment. That is paramount to thrive past the starting line. A mentor who cannot adapt is unable to sufficiently share with you how to navigate in today's world. A compeer incapable of adapting will quickly become a subordinate because they will be unable to maintain "equal rank, status, or ability." Adaptability is as indispensable to the *actiophil* as money is to the bank.

Mindful

To be mindful is to be conscious. This world is filled with distractions pulling you in directions that are foreign to your purpose. People who are mindful enough to recognize overt and subtle attempts to deter them from the proper path will reach the finish line. My parents taught me to look both ways before I cross the street. Life taught me to look both ways before I make a decision. That takes mindfulness, the ability to see beyond what is in front of you, looking left and right before deciding if it's best to move forward or not. This Diamond Quality will save you tons of time and money. Surround yourself with people who are mindful.

Objective

Perhaps one of the most difficult Diamond Qualities is the ability to be objective. *Oxford Dictionary* defines "objective" as "not influenced by personal feelings or opinions in considering and representing facts."[46] As humans, we are prisoners of bias (which is the opposite of being objective). How we think, respond, and act is, in large part, a result of preconditioned filters. No one is exempt from the inclination to view life through preconceived notions or ideas. How Stuff Works reported: "Scientists consider bias to be such a major problem that in recent years, it's become a subject of research itself, in which scholars use statistical analysis and other methods to figure out how often it occurs and why."[47] The comic below from *Chainsawsuit* by Kris Straub perfectly illustrates the human condition of bias[48]:

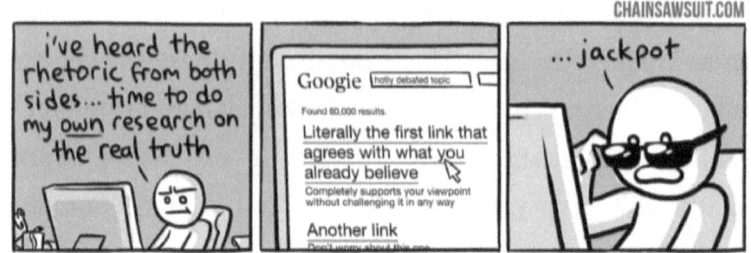

An objective person has the ability to think or act independently of personal feelings or emotions. Although objectivity is difficult to achieve, I list it as a Diamond Quality because of its benefits and usefulness for *actiophils*. When crossing the starting line, you need your mentor or compeer to share advice with you based on truth and reality, not on what will make you feel good. For example, when I released my first book and my friends read through it, I asked them for their thoughts. Expectedly, they gave me good reviews. Then I asked, "What could be better? What can I change for the next version? Which concepts were impactful? Which ideas were too cliché?" If I had not asked those questions, the average person would have provided that perspective constructively. But my Diamond did. Finding mentors and compeers who work toward being objective will hold you accountable and help you reach the finish line.

Noble

To be noble, according to the *Oxford Dictionary*, is "having or showing fine personal qualities or high moral principles."[49] In the example of David Frederick and I both writing a book at the same time, it's important to add that we were writing for the same audience; both of us are Haitian-Americans in our mid-twenties, and we share a similar circle of friends. We could easily have regressed into backbiting, tearing each other down, attempting to discourage each other to inhibit the progress of our books. But we did not. David and I are of noble character and would not dare do that to each other. When you're scouting for a mentor or compeer, look for someone who possesses the fundamental quality of nobility.

Dutiful

Cambridge Dictionary defines dutiful as "(of a person) obedient or (of an action) done because it is necessary or expected."[50] This Diamond Quality may seem like a given. But it is not, or there would be no need for this book. Every year, houses sink into foreclosure, children lie awake in bed with empty stomachs rumbling, young people get hauled to jail because someone did not fulfill their duty. Mentors and compeers that do not respect their own duties will most certainly neglect to urge you to do yours.

Negative Thinking

Growing up, I watched a lot of sports. Mostly basketball with a healthy dose of football. My goal was to be tall and muscular. But people would always tell me that if I lifted weights at a young age, it would stunt my growth, and I believed them. So I did not exercise with anything heavy while in elementary and middle school. By the end of my ninth-grade year, I decided it was time to begin lifting weights, though I was far too skinny to be taken seriously. When the time came for me to choose classes for tenth grade, I listed weight training as my number one elective. I was tired of looking scrawny. People described me as my chest touching my back.

The next school year, I was rife with joy to see Weight Training appear on my official class list! The first day of class was all about rules and safe practices; as the class was winding down, the teacher, (let's call him) Coach Rohan, said these words that shifted the course of our thinking. He said, "In this weight room, there is only one curse word. That is not the f-bomb, the "b" word, or the "s" word. The only word that will not be allowed in this weight room is "can't." That is the last time it will be said without a slap on the neck in return." (This rule was logical because the c-word narrows our attention toward our inadequacies. Confucius, the Chinese philosopher and politician said, "He who says he can and he who says he can't are both usually right."[51])

I remember telling myself, *He is only saying that for now; he'll forget in a couple weeks.* I was wrong. Whenever a student mistakenly said the c-word when lifting heavy weights, the entire class would stop what they were doing. The punishment was a hard slap on the neck—each time! Unfortunately, I was guilty of expressing disbelief in myself on more than one occasion. The result of cursing was painful.

At the time, I thought the "No C-Word Rule" applied only to the weight room. Again, I was wrong. In Coach Rohan's class, the punishment for saying the c-word was physical pain, but in life, the punishment is the suspension of belief in one's own self. The words "I can't" cause the prospect of failure to spread in the mind like an uncontrollable brain tumor.

Likewise, the "tumor" of negative thinking can ravage your emotions and will to succeed.

Imagine if your worst enemy were to hear the vile and deplorable words you say about yourself; they would probably take a vacation from causing you grief. Often, our most harm comes not from our adversary but from ourselves. Fortunately, negative thinking is not a permanent mind state. There is a way out. No one is a permanent slave to the demons of doubt and despair.

The Law of Intentionality

The remedy to the disease of negative thinking is within your power now and can be activated at any time. The solution is in reframing your mindset to become intentional about your thoughts. The question is: How?

John C. Maxell, in his book *The 15 Invaluable Laws of Growth: Live Them and Reach Your Potential*, discusses the Law of Intentional Growth. Although his focus is not directed specifically to negative thinking, I found that following this law has a greater effect on reframing my mindset than most other methods. Maxwell teaches about accidental growth versus intentional growth. Below is his measurement system[52]:

Accidental Growth	Intentional Growth
Plans to Start Tomorrow	Insists on Starting Today
Waits for Growth to Come	Takes Complete Responsibility to Grow
Learns Only from Mistakes	Often Learns before Mistakes
Depends on Good Luck	Relies on Hard Work
Quits Early and Often	Perseveres Long and Hard
Falls into Bad Habits	Fights for Good Habits
Talks Big	Follows Through
Plays it Safe	Takes Risks
Thinks Like a Victim	Thinks Like a Learner
Relies on Talent	Relies on Character
Stops Learning after Graduation	Never Stops Growing

Intentional growth is crucial to the *actiophil*. It is difficult to stumble mistakenly past the starting line. There must be a focused effort to train oneself to adopting a new method of viewing the world. People develop the accidental growth mindset from years of passive living. Whatever thought comes to their mind, they accept. If success comes, "Hurray!" If failure comes, "Oh no!" In either case, they feel life is out of their control. To overcome negative thinking, you must be intentional about your thoughts and actions.

Neuroplasticity

In elementary school, one of my favorite toys to play with was Play-Doh .Whenever the teacher would bring it out, I was like a kid in a proverbial candy shop. Play-doh is a soft, mushy, flexible, and colorful dough. I used it to create little monsters, weird-looking animals, miniature buildings, small cars, or something fun to play with. What I loved most about Play-Doh was the ability to change it at will.

Believe or not, your brain has that same function. In the past, scientists believed the brain develops only during youth. They thought it was incapable of being changed once a person reached adulthood. To their surprise, they were wrong. They discovered that the brain changes through a process now called "neuroplasticity." Neuropsychologist Dr. Celeste Campbell, PsyD, shared, "[Neuroplasticity] refers to the physiological changes in the brain that happen as the result of our interactions with our environment. From the time the brain begins to develop in utero until the day we die, the connections among the cells in our brains reorganize in response to our changing needs."[53] In simpler terms, neuroplasticity is the process through which your brain changes as a result of new experiences. Sentis, a platform to provide psychological and innovative solutions, put it this way:

> *Think of your brain as a dynamic connected, power grid. There are billions of pathways or roads lighting up every time you think, feel, or do something. Some of*

these roads are well traveled. These are our habits. Our established way of thinking, feeling, or doing. Every time we think in a certain way, practice a particular task, or feel a specific emotion, we strengthen this road. It becomes easier for our brain to travel this pathway.

Say we think about things differently, learn a new task, or choose a different emotion; we start carving out a new road. If we keep traveling that road, our brain begins to use that pathway more and this new way of thinking, feeling, or doing eventually becomes second nature. At the same time, the old pathway gets used less and less and weakens. This process of rewiring your brain by forming new connections and weakening old ones is neuroplasticity in action. [54]

This is exciting news for anyone suffering with perpetual negative thoughts. Your brain can change. However, this takes time. Do not expect your brain to do a complete 180-degree turnaround simply because you yelled "I can do it" in the mirror this morning. Every day up until this point, you have been telling yourself something that contributes to how you think and behave. You have literally created some pathways in your brain that engraved negative thought processes into your psyche. To become an *actiophil*, you need to change the direction of these pathways.

You have told yourself the c-word so many times that your brain shifted into a place where positivity goes to die. Maybe the reason you feel hopeless is because you trained your brain to operate as someone who is inadequate, incompetent, and powerless. People treat you like crap because they wired their brains to see you as a tumor on society. It may be difficult to change the minds of others, but you can certainly change your own brain.

Laura Boyd, a brain researcher at the University of British Columbia, states, "One thing is absolutely clear: the best driver of neuroplastic change is your behavior."[55] When you change your habits and way of thinking on day one, your brain shares chemical signaling between brain cells. This fire neurons that only allows for a short-term change. As you continue to intentionally change how you think and behave, those neurons fire up again but now it begins to affect the structure of your brain. As neurologist commonly say, "Neurons that fire together wire together."[56] Your brain will rewire itself into the way you want it to be.

This truth has a large impact on your thought process. Neuroplasticity gives you the power to abandon negative thinking and adopt a positive outlook on the world. This new, positive way of being will give you more courage and willpower to cross the starting line.

I understand this is not an easy task, but honestly, I am thankful for its difficulty. The purpose of this book is not to provide "quick-fix, 7 days guaranteed or your money back solutions." The process of becoming an *actiophil* will transform you into the best version of yourself. But you must first commit to pursuing your own progress. Begin to treat yourself as someone who is worthy of a life headed toward the finish line. You have the power to shape your brain. Don't hesitate. GO!

The Triple I Process

No one is a stranger to struggling through negative emotions and a difficult past; baggage is inherent in the human experience. Although I am not someone who feels deep, negative emotions often, there are times when I feel completely overwhelmed.

During the fall of 2018, I was entrenched in student government work as president. My governing council was facing perilous times due to looming budget cuts, the future of the council, maintaining and managing services for the students, and dealing with unruly colleagues. Moreover, graduate schoolwork was burying me alive. Given I was going through financial setbacks at that time, I did not have the funds to purchase textbooks for class. This caused my grades to nose dive, creating a real possibility of failing that class and pushing my graduation back a full year. At the time, I was also in the process of writing this book. My goal was to finish writing by the end of the year so it could be ready for what I hoped would be graduation in May of 2019. In addition to all of those stress factors, I had commitments in the community that required attention.

With all of these roads converging into my life, the hands of stress and anxiety placed a tight grip around my neck. I could have collapsed under the pressure of my heavy plate. But then I remembered the words of my good friend Sam Tarell: "If there is too much on your plate, you can feed more than just you."[57] Those words shifted my thought process. I decided not to wallow in negative thoughts. Instead, I evolved through what I call the "Triple I Process"—Identify, Introduce, and Invest.

Identify:

You must first understand that you are not your negative emotions; you simply possess those emotions at the time. Once you recognize that you are independent of negative thoughts, it becomes easier to acknowledge them. In writing about methods of dealing with negative thoughts, Senior Psychologist of Seleni Institute, Patricia Harteneck, PhD, advocates for recognizing thought distortions as the first step. She encourages you to recognize these four common thought distortions:

1. Black-and-white thinking: This causes you to view the world through a strictly good or bad, negative or positive, point of view.
2. Personalizing: You attribute all the bad things around you to your doing;
3. Filter thinking: You adopt the glass is half-empty, all things are negative view of the world.

4. Catastrophizing: You think the sky is falling (mentally), and the absolute worst is doomed to happen.[58]

To overcome those thought distortions, Dr. Harteneck writes you should: give yourself a break from negative thoughts, take a break from judgement, practice gratitude, focus on your strengths, and seek out professional support. [59]

> *Once you recognize that you are independent of negative thoughts, it becomes easier to acknowledge them.*

Introduce:

After recognizing I was slipping into that slump of stress during the fall of 2018, I decided to lean on my Dynamic Diamond (see the previous chapter). I introduced my situation to people around me capable of helping and then invited them to introduce solutions. No one-size-fits-all advice could have reversed my situation. I spoke with mentors, compeers, mentees, my professors, advisors, financial experts, and more. They introduced me to a new way of thinking, different habits, advice based on experience, a listening ear. Had I not introduced those negative emotions to positive counsel, I would have remained in an overwhelmed state.

Invest:

As we've learned, neuroplasticity gives your brain the ability to change. In light of this, there are three major investments you can make:

1. Invest in treasure, not in trash. If you feed yourself bad energy through social media garbage, emotionally draining conversations, self-pity, and so on, that energy will get locked inside of you. If you instead invest in positive media, healthy conversations, and self-encouragement, you can change the tides in your favor.
2. Invest in healthy relationships. We are social creatures. We become who we are constantly surrounded by. As the behavioral scientist Steve Maraboli says, "If you hang out with chickens, you're going to cluck, and if you hang out with eagles, you're going to fly."[60]
3. Invest in your mental health. Becoming an *actiophil* at the risk of your sanity is dangerous. It is okay to rest, take a day off, watch funny videos, or go on vacation. Whatever brings you into a place of peace, go there when times get too rough.

Excuses

My dream, as a child, of becoming an NBA basketball star crowded out all other dreams. I remember watching the Miami Heat battle the Detroit Pistons in the 2006 NBA Eastern Conference finals for a chance to compete in the NBA finals to become world champions. This was only the second time in my life that I had watched live basketball, and my heart skipped a few beats. The first time was the year prior on June 6, 2005, when the Miami Heat lost to the Detroit Pistons in Game 7. Now a year later, my eyes were glued to the television in anticipation of Miami Heat avenging their fall last year. Miami won the first game, then lost the second one. Dwyane Wade, star player for the Heat, was determined not to lose this year to the same team. The Detroit Pistons were their proverbial Goliath.

Detroit was a ferocious team. Two years prior, they had defeated Kobe Bryant and the Los Angeles Lakers to become NBA champions. The year after that, they defeated the Heat en route to the NBA Finals. Now Detroit was looking to roll over the Heat again. As a young team, the Miami Heat lacked championship experience as an organization, and, given the dominance of Detroit, they were an underdog in the fight. Fortunately for the Heat, this was not the first time Dwyane Wade had been an underdog. Growing up, he had survived a rocky childhood. At a young age, his parents split up, and his mother won custody. In a special two-hour episode of "Oprah's Lifeclass," Dwyane Wade recalled: "Early on in my life, I grew up with my mom...My mom was on drugs and my family was in the gang environment, so it was a rough childhood. [At the age of nine] I moved with my father. I got an opportunity to be a kid. If I would have stayed [with my Mom]... I would have been next in line to sell drugs, to join the gang."[61]

Adversity has always lived at the doorstep of Dwyane Wade's life. He had every reason to live an average and unremarkable life and a sea of excuses to drown out hope for the future. But he decided to press his foot on the neck of hopelessness. Dwyane Wade overcame, and he carried that same mentality into the 2006 Eastern Conference finals. The mountains seemed too large to climb, and the Detroit Pistons were no scrubs. But Dwyane was no stranger to slaying Goliaths. He eventually led the Miami Heat to defeat the Pistons. Weeks afterward, Wade and Miami Heat overcame the Dallas Mavericks and won the first championship for the franchise in its history. Wade abandoned excuses and became a finals champion and won the most valuable player award. After a devastating injury, he went on to win a gold medal for the United States. He won two more championships in 2012 and 2013.

What is preventing you from crossing the starting line? What are your excuses?

It is important to note there are distinct differences between making an excuse and being genuinely unable to cross the starting line. *Cambridge Dictionary* defines excuse as "a false reason that you give to explain why you do something…to give false reasons why you cannot do something."[62] The operative word in that definition is "false." An excuse can be reasonable but not genuine.

Below is a short list of common excuses gathered by The Behance Team, manager of the Behance Creative Network, the 99% productivity think tank, and the Action Method project management application[63]:

1. I don't have enough time
2. I'm afraid of failure
3. I'm not inspired
4. I need to find balance in my work and home life

5. It's not original enough
6. I'm afraid of the competition
7. It's not the right moment to do it
8. I have to plan everything first
9. The idea isn't polished enough yet
10. I have young children

Each of these excuses can be legitimate. Imagine if I am a single father with three children, work two jobs, and have a desire to open a restaurant. Excuse numbers 1, 4, and 10 apply directly to my situation. Even if my desire to open the restaurant is pressing at my heart, I must take into consideration the responsibilities I committed myself to. Abandoning my responsibilities would be both reckless and foolish. However, I would argue that 1, 4, 7, 8, and 10 could possibly be legitimate reasons for not moving forward. But as an *actiophil*, you may still want to cross the starting line, and I am going to teach you how:

1. I don't have enough time

Yes, you do have time. Regardless of who you are, where you come from, and what you have, there will always be enough time to start. How? Usually, when someone uses the "I don't have enough time" reason, they say it in reference to not having time to be immersed in the idea *plus* maintain the same lifestyle. However, for most endeavors, it is not absolutely necessary to divest from your normal activities to cross the starting line.

> *I do not wear my failures as a badge of honor, but I realize those shortcomings became ladders toward a higher calling.*

In the above example, it would be extremely difficult to open a restaurant, be a single father, and keep both jobs. But it would be feasible to keep both jobs and ask friends to come over to your house one Saturday a month for a paid dinner. If the food is good, they will want to come back. Every month, ask them to bring a new friend. Although that is not a restaurant, you are gaining experience running your own operation, which will prepare you for greater steps in the future.

You must look for windows in your schedule to cross the starting line. Trust me, if you create a time-conducive strategy, you will certainly find time.

2. I'm afraid of failure

If you listen to anyone who is moderately successful, they will tell you that failure is a prerequisite to success. At the beginning of this book, I described a few failures I faced after crossing the starting line. Believe me, I do not wear my failures as a badge of honor, but I realize those shortcomings became ladders toward a higher calling. Some say that F.A.I.L. means

"First Attempt In Learning." I disagree. If that is what fail means, we need to change the definition of sail and tail. S.A.I.L. would mean second attempt in learning and T.A.I.L. would mean third attempt in learning. I would argue that fail means "Future Always Involves Learning." The lessons you will learn through failure will strengthen, embolden, and empower you to break past the starting line.

3. I'm not inspired

This world is a bleak and dark place. Some people are born, live in starvation throughout their life, get sick, then die. Others experience the full glories of life, get into an accident, then spend the rest of their life dependent on others. It's not surprising why so many people are not inspired. There are too many scenarios where your hopes and aspirations can descend into the flames of defeat. Then why cross the starting line?

The answer is simple: You are already defeated if you never try. As the Hall of Fame hockey player Wayne Gretzky famously said, "You miss 100% of the shots you don't take."[64] My goal isn't to force you to be inspired but to encourage you to be rational. A lack of inspiration can only bring you lower. But moving past the starting line gives you room to grow.

4. I need to find balance in my work and home life

It goes without saying—balance is I-M-P-O-R-T-A-N-T! When I asked Google "how to find balance," within .51 of a second, about 1,040,000,000 results popped up. I came across articles from "How to Find a Work-Life Balance in Medical School" to "How to Balance Being Mom and Being Yourself." On the twenty-fourth page of google, I found an article titled "How to Find Balance between Change & Acceptance." That is important. But it's pushed so far back because of the sheer number of people who covered the topic of finding balance. People are struggling up a steep mountain—whether it be emotional, financial, relational, mental, spiritual, or internal—toward the peak. Here is how to make balance possible:

Traditional balance as we know it is difficult because of false ideas about how to reach it. Balance is more than a moment in time or a point in history. *True balance occurs when your priorities and your energy are in alignment with each other.* Taking action has to be embedded into your balanced structure. Losing weight or changing eating habits or going back to school or traveling the world—whatever your goals are, they have to be in your list of priorities. If you are taking action based on an afterthought rather than putting energy toward the necessary initial thoughts, balance will be difficult to find.

> *True balance occurs when your priorities and your energy are in alignment with each other.*

5. It's not original enough and 6. I'm afraid of the competition

Guess what? Competition is afraid of you too. For the next one hundred years, we will be studying how Netflix destroyed Blockbuster, Uber killed the Taxi industry, and Instagram is taking out digital cameras. These emergent companies have put the world on notice. There is ALWAYS room for innovation and creativity. There will always be market share for the new idea.

The famed painter, sculptor, poet, and stage designer Pablo Picasso, is credited with saying, "Good artist copy, great artist steal."[65] I must confess, I love Pablo Picasso's paintings, but I disagree with his quote. Concerns of inauthenticity are appropriate. Originality is desired. The only plans that are totally crushed by competition and not original enough are the plans that never see the light of day.

7. It's not the right moment to do it

The Behance Team put it this way: "With images of fame and success dancing in our heads, we set the bar too high, fail to make the grade, and quit because we're discouraged."[66] The future can be scary. In many cases, not because of potential tragedy but because of potential fortune. It may be difficult to cross the starting line and go back into the dating scene after coming from an abusive relationship. Comparing the person you were with prior to the person of your dreams can be daunting and intimidating. Of course, with good reason.

What is the solution? Should you think small? Absolutely not! I encourage you to think big. Imagine the best possible scenario. Place the highest standard for yourself. The solution is not to shrink the vision but instead to create small goals that lead up to the larger goal. For example, if you are that person who moved out of the abusive relationship, don't immediately return to the dating scene; your wounds are too fresh. Instead, find people who once were abused as well but are now in ideal relationships. Befriend them and learn how they were healed of those deep wounds. Doing this will help you get off ground zero and into a better place to love again. If you are genuine about crossing the starting line, practice climbing hills before you endeavor to climb the mountain. From there, the right time will reveal itself.

8. I have to plan everything first and 9. The idea isn't polished enough yet

No you don't have to plan anything first. Nor do your ideas have to be polished like a sculpture. Planning is important. But life changes so dramatically after you cross the starting line that a plan that is too thorough and detailed would combat the gift of flexibility.

You need room for change. You must have space to update your strategy. As you are moving, the world is moving around you. The excuse of "planning everything first" is understandable but not necessary. The most important thing to polish is the lens through which you view the world. If your lens is gloomy and pessimistic, every problem will seem like an impossible obstacle, even if you have a "plan" to get past it. But if your lens is polished to be hopeful and optimistic, you will work diligently to overcome.

> *If you are genuine about crossing the starting line, practice climbing hills before you endeavor to climb the mountain.*

10. I have young children

Take care of your children! As far as I can tell, that is the most important job someone can do. Never compromise on your duty to your children. Everything else comes in a far second. With that being said, what is your final goal? What is your finish line? How can you be the best possible parent while crossing the starting line?

One possible solution is to cross the line with your children. Don't make decisions that would jeopardize their upbringing and your success. Get your Diamond involved. How can they help? Look persistently for solutions so your children do not become your biggest problem.

To fall victim to excuses is to chain your feet together and throw the key as far as possible. There will always be reasons not to start. But there will *not* always be opportunities to start. People who are accustomed to settling in front of the starting line will always find problems for every solution, while the actioiphil will find a solution to every problem. Excuses can be real and genuine, but they do not have to hold you hostage. I encourage you to cross the starting line with wisdom to overcome what many people allow to overwhelm them.

Ignorance

Two of the most dangerous people in the world are the person who doesn't know anything but is content and the person who thinks they know everything. The first person is trapped in a cage of oblivion but thinks they are free, while the second person lives on an island of knowledge but thinks that island is the entire world. Both are victims of the plague of ignorance.

Before I continue, allow me to address the word "ignorant." Society views the word as a negative term, but in reality that is not always the case. Ignorance is defined as a "lack of knowledge or information." By that definition, everyone is ignorant about many things. For example, a neural physicist may be ignorant about architecture, while an English professor may be ignorant about South African constitutional law. Simply because you lack knowledge in one field does not mean you are devoid of knowledge in all areas. Crossing the starting line into an unknown space is difficult. If you never been on the journey to the finish line, there is a gap in knowledge between what you know and what you need to know to succeed. That gap, which is called ignorance, prevents many people from taking action. That is understandable. However, you can still GO. My goal is not to encourage you to cross the starting line despite ignorance but to cross by overcoming ignorance.

I am not writing this book because I know everything about starting. There are people who are far more equipped than I—people who crossed the starting line more times than I have attempted. But guess what? I wrote this book. Not them. With the knowledge I received from experience, research I have done to validate what I'm sharing, I closed the gap between what I know and what I need to know. That is why I crossed the starting line. If you lack knowledge that would prevent you from reaching the finish line, this is what to do:

Become Curious

In the world of the *actiophil*, ignorance is not a viable excuse. The cure to ignorance is curiosity. Sophie von Stumm, Benedikt Hell, and Tomas Chammorro-Premuzic published a study titled *The Hungry Mind: Intellectual Curiosity Is the Third Pillar of Academic Performance*. In their research, they found that "a 'hungry mind' is a core determinant of individual differences in academic achievement."[67] In other words, your level of curiosity directly affects your academic performance. This research suggests curiosity can give you the educational edge over those who are less curious.

This study is world changing because it puts the ball in your hands. You have the ability to direct the trajectory of your knowledge base. Although the study is specific to academic achievement, it is important to note that academic achievement is closely correlated to intelligence. This matters a great deal, because research from American Friends of Tel Aviv University turns the popular phrase "it is not what you know but who you know" on its head. Their researchers found "When intelligence and socioeconomic background are pitted directly against one another, intelligence is a more accurate predictor of future career success."[68]

There is a lot to unpack in those two studies. Here is the simplest way to think about it: curiosity kills ignorance, which in turn increases intelligence. The best predictor of success is intelligence. Therefore, those who are curious place themselves in a better position to succeed. Dear *actiophil*, not only will curiosity help you cross the starting line, it will also place you in a better position to reach the finish line.

Ian Leslie, who is a London-based journalist and author of critically acclaimed books about human behavior writes in his book *Curious: The Desire to Know and Why Your Future Depends on It*: "The truly curious will be increasingly in demand. Employers are looking for people who can do more than follow procedures competently or respond to requests; who have a strong intrinsic desire to learn, solve problems and ask penetrating questions. They may be difficult to manage at times, these individuals, for their interests and enthusiasms can take them along unpredictable paths, and they don't respond well to being told what to think. But for the most part, they will be worth the difficulty."[69]

Ian's writing combats the idea that curiosity killed the cat. Interestingly enough, curiosity made the cat stronger. For us humans, curiosity will empower and embolden us. This begs the question of how to become curious. What do curious people do?

Seek Diverse Perspectives

People are interesting. As individuals, we are extremely unique. It will take a lifetime to know someone as well as you know yourself. The ability to converse, engage, and learn about someone with a different background is a gift. At a leadership conference I attended, the organizers brought in a speaker to teach us life lessons to never forget. One of those lessons was about the importance of meeting people of distinct backgrounds. The speaker said that whenever she goes to a networking event, the first people she speaks to are those who dress differently from her, speak another language, have a different accent, are from another country, and so on. "Those people," she noted, "not only will have a different perspective you can learn from, they also have a network you could tap into across the world."

It's easy to converse with someone with whom you went to school, shared the same major, worked in the same company, or grew up on the same block. Both of your experiences, for the most part, would have a lot of overlap.

Being intentional about finding and interacting with people who have led a life different from your own opens you up to a new world. There is a good chance those people have insights and perspectives that are foreign to you. Jordan Peterson, a Canadian professor of psychology at the University of Toronto, wrote as the ninth rule in his book *12 Rules for Life: An Anecdote to Chaos*, "Assume that the person you're listening to might know something you don't."[70] Curiosity would put you in the position to seek those diverse perspectives while also helping you learn new things. That knowledge and network will open doors to make crossing the starting line easier.

Questions! Questions! Questions!

From pre-k to high school, the education system told you what they felt you needed to know to be successful. If it had been up to us as children, we would not have asked for over a decade of math or countless years of science or the two-hour lectures on social studies. We would have requested eight hours of recess nonstop. But thankfully, we did not get what we wanted. Once you graduate from high school and/or college, you are no longer compelled to take classes on subjects that do not pique your interest. However, chances are that everything you learned in primary and secondary education is not enough to sustain you to live a rewarding life. This is where you need curiosity. Remember, curiosity kills ignorance. What knowledge do you need to cross the starting line? What do you need to know to avoid crashing and burning? What subject must you have a working knowledge in before you start?

After you have those answers, that is where "Questions! Questions! Questions!" come in.

You have people, Google, books, YouTube, and, if you are desperate, Bing. Ask questions! Ignorance is no longer a viable excuse in the twenty-first century. While you are asking questions, actually wait for the answers. Have those answers inform your decision-making.

> *Do not settle for face value. Curiosity will drive you to venture below the surface into a world of wisdom.*

Don't Settle for the Surface

The French moralist and essayist Joseph Joubert exquisitely said, "It is better to debate a question without settling it than to settle a question without debating it."[71] Curiosity is more than seeking out an answer to a question. Curiosity strives to go on a journey for an answer. That journey involves internal debate, which leads to a deeper understanding. When working toward decreasing ignorance and increasing intelligence, you should feel discontent with surface-level answers. In much the same way that two people argue and debate over politics, philosophy, and/or sports, you should question what you know and what you are learning. True knowledge is found in the places few people look.

In the book *Rise Up and Salute the Sun*, Suzy Kassem, poet and artist of Egyptian origin, wrote powerful words that illustrate the need to go deeper: "I have been finding treasures in places I did not want to search. I have been hearing wisdom from tongues I did not want to listen. I have been finding beauty where I did not want to look. And I have learned so much from journeys I did not want to take. Forgive me, O Gracious One; for I have been closing my ears and eyes for too long. I have learned that miracles are only called miracles because they are often witnessed by only those who can see through all of life's illusions. I am ready to see what really exists on [the] other side, what exists behind the blinds, and taste all the ugly fruit instead of all that looks right, plump and ripe."[72]

Do not settle for face value. Curiosity will drive you to venture below the surface into a world of wisdom.

SUCCESS

On the one-inch wall that carries obvious crippling bricks such as fear, laziness, and negative thinking, the brick named success sticks out like a sore thumb. It looks like a mistake. But in reality, some people do not cross the starting line because they are afraid of the finish line. The journey toward success is certainly difficult, but the life after the finish line, for many people, can be even more challenging. Those who are aware of this may intentionally forego the journey to avoid the pain of victory.

While I served as Senator of Communications and Journalism in the student government at FIU, a countless number of people demanded I should run for president the following year. I kindly told each of them no. Although, I was well qualified for the position, I rejected all of their suggestions. I understood that success does not always taste like candy. Every victory comes with responsibility. In Luke 14 of the Bible, Jesus said, "'Suppose one of you wants to build a tower. Won't you first sit down and estimate the cost to see if you have enough money to complete it? For if you lay the foundation and are not able to finish it, everyone who sees it will ridicule you, saying, "This person began to build and wasn't able to finish."'"[73]

I counted the cost of the presidency, and I calculated that it would be expensive. I understood success meant I would be the most committed, use a lot of emotional and intellectual energy, serve as the chief servant, face rapidly rising expectations, and take on a tenfold increase in responsibility to the students. Those were the ingredients to a successful presidency. I did not want to start a tower that I could not finish or maintain. Those same thoughts that caused me to say no to all of those people may be similar to what is holding you back. Below are a few examples of the cost of success for different scenarios:

Success: Getting married
Cost: You have to share everything

Success: Going to college
Cost: According to www.debt.org, the average student debt in 2017 was $37,172.[74]

Success: Eat Healthy

Cost: Food that is healthy is usually more expensive

Success: Travel the World

Cost: Spend less time with family and close friends

Success: Become Wealthy

Cost: Everyone think you are a bank and no longer see you as a person

Success: Win a High Political seat

Cost: you lose privacy

Success can be expensive. For that reason, some people would rather subsist than incur the price of their accomplishment. My thought process was the same when people approached me about running for president of the student government…until a sobering conversation with my brother, David Noel. I remember telling him in a joking manner how people wanted me to submit my application for the position. I was expecting him to laugh with me. But instead, he gazed deep into my eyes with the most serious look and asked, "Why not?" Then, there was a long pause. I proceeded to echo all the excuses I could muster. But as my mouth moved, I realized it was misaligned with my heart. At that moment, I realized that the setbacks that could make the experience negative were necessary to make a meaningful difference in the lives of thousands of people. The reward of stepping into greatness superseded the ease of comfortability.

That same cost from the aforementioned success paled in comparison to the reward of success:

Success: Getting married
Benefit: Commitment to someone for better, for worse, for richer, for poorer, in sickness and in health, to love and to cherish, till death do the two of you part.

Success: Going to college
Benefit: A report by Georgetown University found that, on average, college graduates earn $1 million more than non-graduates do over a lifetime.[75]

Success: Eat Healthy
Benefit: Health is wealth. If you eat unhealthy food to save money, you will spend a lot more money in medical bills later

Success: Travel the World
Benefit: You escape the monotony of everyday life, and increase your communication and social skills

Success: Become Wealthy
Benefit: You have freedom of choice

Success: Win a High Political seat
Benefit: You can change the political landscape and make life-changing decisions for millions of people

Dear *actiophil*, do not let the cost of success blind you from the benefits. Looking back now, I am thrilled to have taken the leap and throw my hat in the ring for president. We accomplished a myriad of things for the student body—from creating internship and job opportunities to collecting hundreds of pounds of food for students in need to improving student safety and even having students register to vote in the past general elections. Moreover, I had the opportunity to advocate for FIU in the state capitol and in Washington D.C. as well. Those feats would not have been possible had I allowed the strains of success to keep me from crossing the starting line.

Let's examine another reason why success can be scary and how to overcome.

> Do not let the cost of success blind you from the benefits.

Upkeep

During my high school years, my parents did not drive me to school, nor did I take the yellow school bus; I always took public transportation. Those four years of my life, I caught the bus everywhere, whether to the mall, church, a friend's house, or the movies. It was normal for me. Until I got my first car. That was a huge step for me in my life. Now it took not an hour to go to the movies but fifteen minutes. Although the car was a 2003 blue Chevy Cavalier, I drove it like it was a brand new Mercedes. After getting that car, I never wanted to catch the bus again under any circumstance. If the car was in the shop, I would not leave my house to go anywhere unless I was getting picked up. I scoffed at the idea of catching the bus.

A couple years later, the blue Chevy began overheating and coughing smoke every three miles that led to my dad selling the vehicle. I upgraded to a 2006 Ford F-150. Then, years after that, I began driving a 2011 Nissan Altima. At this point, if anything goes wrong with the Nissan, downgrading to another 2006 or 2003 car would make me hide my face in shame. Not because those cars couldn't get me from point A to point B but because of the symbolic loss of status. That is the problem with keeping up with the Jones. Once you reach a higher status of whatever, you expect yourself and others to maintain or exceed that status. Given this reality, many people would prefer to remain low on the totem pole so they do not have to meet higher expectations.

The problem of keeping my image polished, for the most part, is self-imposed. No one has a gun to my head forcing me to only purchase cars that look better or are more expensive than the previous ones. Wanting to constantly upgrade car stems from an insecurity of what others will think if I downgrade. The solution is a truth that is hard to swallow. Success is like the stock market. Sometimes there are bull markets, other times there are bear markets. In other words, a constant incline of success does not exist. Below is what I call the Reality Graph (figure 3):

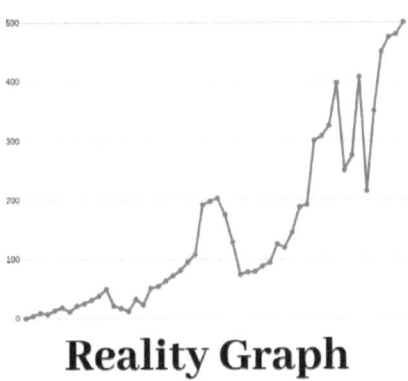

Reality Graph

Figure 3

Now look at the stark difference between the Reality Graph and the Society's Perception Graph:

Society's Perception Graph

Both are displaying the same person on the same path. But one depicts reality while the other shows what society sees.

The Society's Perception Graph can also be coined as the What I Wish for Graph. But the truth remains—a constant incline of success does not exist. Therefore, you do not need to fear having to maintain or increase your status; no one can manage to go up without going down from time to time. On my website, jeffersonnoel.com, I wrote an article titled "Caution: The Road to Purpose is Slippery." That article was inspired by the African Proverb: "Do not look where you fell but where you slipped." I wrote, "As you learn, grow, explore, create, and expand your horizons, failure is inevitable. You will come up short. Your expectations may not be met and people may abandon you. But your focus should not be on the outcome (per se), but on the mental process preceding the outcome."[76]

Dear *actiophil*, do not live according to the expectations society places on you for what success looks like. Go through the struggle and pain of success. Do not let someone's ungrounded opinion of you determine your behavior. Do not let false expectations of yourself keep you from starting. Cross the starting line regardless of how many times you have to get up before and after the finish line.

Become a Target

In politics, there is a term called opposition research. It is defined as "investigation into the dealings of political opponents, typically in order to discredit them publicly."[77] The entire job of these researchers is to find any and everything bad on a political candidate in order to expose that person publicly. Every distasteful comment, unhinged moment, parking and/or speeding ticket, corrupt deal, or anything negative someone has to say about the candidate will be uncovered.

> *The key to overcome being a target is to focus on your target.*

Imagine someone revealing to the world how you behaved on your worst day and painting that picture of you to the public. You would melt with embarrassment. That occurs often but this does not stop folks from running for office.

Celebrities are constantly harpooned by paparazzi following their every move; conversation among friends, if leaked, becomes public discourse. TMZ is always on the prow looking to close the gap between public and private life. Sadly enough, these targets do not stop at celebrities or politicians; anyone in a leadership position is subject to ridicule and judgement.

The sad truth is—*actiophils* are not safe from the pointed finger of society. To do anything meaningful is to risk the disparagement of others. People will always have something negative to say. Especially with the advent of social media, we see the ugliest side of our neighbors. Although people can and do reinvent themselves on the internet, many choose to be a troll. They elect to use oil as a medium to spread fire instead of driving the world forward. The fear of becoming a target once you cross the starting line is not unfounded. But thankfully there is a solution.

The key to overcome being a target is to focus on your target. A YouTube video named "Dream - Motivational Video"—a compilation of Eric Thomas, Les Brown, and Will Smith empowering and motivating the watcher—has approximately nine thousand dislikes. This means nine thousand people intentionally went out of their way to express their displeasure about the video. That is a lot of people, and I am sure there are many more people who were displeased by the video and did not press the dislike button. Imagine if the gentleman who posted the video, Mateusz, looked at all the disapproval and decided never to publish a video like that again. He would be foolish. Since publishing "Dream - Motivational Video" in 2013, he has also published many more videos that have accrued millions of views, hundreds of thousands of likes, and tens of thousands of dislikes.

If Mateusz had focused only on the nine thousand dislikes, he would have been blinded to the five hundred fifty-five thousand likes. Also, his attention would have been drawn away from the comments posted under his video such as:

- "I watching this video many times since several years ago, and still inspiring me today."
- "his video saved my life so many times ……"

- "This video has a special place in my heart. Getting emotional every single time. Keep fighting. - Merry Christmas <3"[78]

These comments highlight the impact of that video. Although nine-thousand said no, many more people said yes. The folks behind these comments, and all the other "yes" people are where the energy should be directed to.

Dear *actiophil*, focus on your target. Although people may be aiming at you to bring you down, let them waste their time. When I was president of the student government, some people despised my existence because of my position. One person was particularly set on "taking me down." I was warned and cautioned to tread lightly while around this person. I heeded that warning, but I never allowed their ill will to interfere with my plans. While they were set on destroying me, I was set on building bridges of opportunity for those I served. No one can look backward and forward at the same time. I chose to be purpose-oriented and mission driven, and I encourage you to do the same.

Section 2

Your Greatest Resource is Your Passion

Your first question after reading the title of this section is most likely "How can I find my passion?" For many people, this pressing question has no easy answer. Passion is not a tangible object that can be found under your bed. Your passion can stem from an experience or it can bubble up from the depths of your being. Regardless of how it reached you, discovering your passion is vital. Forbes Coaches Council, a group of top business and career coaches, shared questions to ask in order to discover your passion, such as:

- What Was I Like When I Felt The Freest?
- What Would I Do If I Didn't Have To Work?

- What Do I Daydream About?
- What Do Other People Say I'm Passionate About?
- What Makes Me Lose Track Of Time?[79]

These are good questions, but you should not stop there. Notice all those questions start with "What." For those who feel their passion is leaning toward people, here are a different set of questions to ask:

- Who am I around when I feel the freest?
- Who would I be if I'm not influenced by others?
- Who would benefit from my outreach?
- Who would suffer if I don't extend myself to help?

The same can be done for "Where" as well. *Passion is a mysterious feeling of joy mixed with determination toward a desired outcome.* You are not obliged to limit the scope of your passion to someone's opinion. Your passion, which will propel you past the starting line, is uniquely yours. Your passion does not require permission.

The first thing many people do when they think of a great idea is to tell the whole world then wait with bated breath for the nations to marvel with joy through encouragement, funding, and networks for this idea to come into existence. Unfortunately, that is rarely the case. Usually, our idea makes no impact when first expressed. The world rarely bends its ears to listen and take action

on this "great idea."

In July 2016, I conceived of a social organization called Barbershop Speaks. When the idea first crept into my head, my brain juices began exploding with possibilities of expanding to different cities, states, and even around the world. My goal was to spread the organization as quickly as possible, and I hoped each person I told would see the same vision. Unfortunately, that was not the case. Many people gave me their thumbs up but never gave me their hands to make it happen. People exclaimed, "Jeff, this is one of the best ideas I've ever heard." But I had to pull teeth to get them to attend one event. People on social media did back flips at the notion of Barbershop Speaks, but when the time came for the events, they share or invite a soul and left the weight of the marketing on me.

Consequently, I realized my passion—not money or people—was the fuel for the project. My unwavering desire to succeed got the job done. If I had waited for all the people who thought it was a good idea to help me make it possible, I would still be in position at the starting line, not knowing life had already declared GO!

Passion vs Pessimism

I speak of passion as a resource because of the immense value it brings to everything it accomplishes. Often, passion can be detected almost like an odor. It can also be contagious and spread like a pathogen. In that same breath, the opposite is true as well; pessimism can follow someone like a shadow and can be spread like a plague. Some people's only passion in life is pessimism. They relish negative phrases like "You can't do that…If it could've been done, somebody would've done it by now, but especially not you…Trust me, you will embarrass yourself…" For the person who makes it their mission to spread seeds of doubt, progression is their kryptonite, and another story of failure is their daily bread. And the white flag is their symbol of strength.

When you're fighting to become an *actiophil*, crossing the line starting despite these negative people is a great feat. When they vomit their negative thoughts on you, their goal is not only to convey that your idea is bad but also to convince you that your passion is misdirected. They want your energy to go toward what won't threaten their comfort. They don't mind you being "great" as long as they are great first. They have no problem with you making a lot of money as long as they're making more money. These passion-sucking parasites secretly desire the same thing as the *actiophil*. They want to enlarge their reach, but they think the only way to achieve greatness is by making everyone smaller.

Therefore, when you find something worth starting, do not put all your hope in the approval of others. Place faith in the "why" it needs to get done. That "why" will drive you much further than money or people. Whenever all your resources are near depleted and yes is starting to become no, your passion will become the engine and the fuel.

> *You are blessed with a burden of passion. Use it to GO.*

In the early 1700s, a man was born by the name of John Wesley. He was raised under a mantle of faith. His father was a priest, and his mother taught him and his eighteen siblings morality and religion as a cornerstone of their life. As he aged, he experienced a moment where his heart was "strangely warmed."[80] After that, his passion for his faith grew arms and legs. John Wesley went on to become an itinerant preacher. As the United Methodist Church website puts it, Wesley had risen for sixty years at four o'clock in the morning, and for fifty years had preached every morning at five....he preached twice each day, and often thrice or four times.[81] Many estimated John Wesley traveled forty-five hundred English miles every year, mostly upon horseback.

John Wesley's passion was palpable: at the age of eighty-six, he wrote in his journal, "Laziness is slowly creeping in. There is an increasing tendency to stay in bed after five-thirty in the morning."[82] He was committed. His drive was unparalleled and unwavering. Even at the age of eighty-six, passion remained his greatest resource.

Where is your passion? Once you find it, use that fire to burst past the starting line. You are blessed with a burden of passion. Use it to GO.

Filter Your Energy through Your Value System

When I started my first business, Noel's Healthy Living, I was young, hopeful, and determined. As I put together strategies for the best business practices, I visited other high performing businesses that were similar to mine. These places had teams working for them and customers constantly walking in and out the doors. This amazed me! *I will become a money magnet*, I secretly thought to myself.

But as I began to visit more shops, I realized many of the most profitable businesses were cheating their customers, unbeknownst to the patrons. In the shops, for instance, there was a protein shake that needed a full scoop of protein powder to receive the proper serving of protein, but these shops were only tossing half a scoop into the mix. Since the taste was indistinguishable, the customers did not notice. These were bad business practices.

When you cross the starting line, there will always be shortcuts, alleyways, boosters, and people telling you how to finish faster. If you are not disciplined, you may sell your integrity for an easy pass. Be careful with too much ambition, because it may cause you to go morally blind. In an effort to become wealthy beyond imagination, resurrect your marriage, pay for school, and/or graduate on time; do not lose sight of your values. What good is it to cross the starting line if it means becoming corrupt and compromising your sacred beliefs?

Many politicians leave their constituency in the mud and mire simply because they would rather serve the interest of the highest bidder. Maybe at the beginning of their career, they saw themselves as a beacon of hope for their community; but the weight of pressure to "hold the seat" got in the way of truly making a positive difference. The same can be said of couples in a relationship. Perhaps everything started off perfectly but the burden of "looking good together" became the central focus rather than each other. Whatever values you start with, you must finish with as well.

Power Steps vs Baby Steps

Humans are goal-oriented creatures. We are in a constant state of desire. Although we have, we still want more. Just enough is too little, and too much is close to enough. Our innate need to want more can be harmful. Some people are fueled by greed; they will leave no stone unturned until the most vulnerable are exploited for the little they have. Those people are not *actiophils*. On the other hand, there are some who have an insatiable desire for more that create fields of opportunity for themselves and those around them.

> I define Power Steps as "a calculated march toward a particular goal that edifies everyone on the pathway."

For as long as I can remember, I've always worn a different brand of eyes from most of my peers. I tend to empathize with others more easily. Every time I would take a shower, I'd come up with an elaborate plan about how to end world hunger, find a home for the orphan, bind the emotional wounds of the broken, and educate the unschooled. I know those seem like wicked, unsolvable problems, but my mind would always lead me there. People would label me as a dreamer, idealist, or an irrational motivational thinker. For those who didn't want to discourage me, they said to simply take baby steps toward lofty goals.

"Baby steps?" I would ask. How can I take baby steps toward such ambitious goals? It would take me an eternity to reach one-eighth of my mission. Baby steps are for those who want to go from a C to a B in cooking class, or for a weight loss goal of ten pounds in two years. But taking baby steps is not ideal for a person who desires to radically transform the world. So I defied the baby-steps suggestion. I decided to head the opposite direction and take **Power Steps**! Taking baby steps is defined as "mak[ing] progress on something in small increments." I define Power Steps as "a calculated march toward a particular goal that edifies everyone on the pathway."

Ellen Johnson Sirleaf, the world's first elected black female president and Africa's first elected female head of state, famously said, "If your dreams don't scare you, they are not big enough."[83] Power Steps are for those who Steve Jobs called "the crazy ones, the misfits, the rebels, the troublemakers, the round pegs in the square holes...the ones who are crazy enough to think that they can change the world."[84] Power Steps are all about intention.

Baby ideas require Baby Steps. However, your passion requires Power Steps. Drew, founder of the Build Your Own Brand Retreat said, "There are many things that can be done, but you must focus your energy on the steps that will yield the most fruit."[85] Movement does not always equate to progress. Staff writer for LifeHacker, Patrick Allan, wrote, "A rocking horse keeps moving but doesn't make any progress."[86] People who take Power Steps move forward with intention. They calculate the effectiveness of each step and try not to repeat fruitless steps. They turn on the GPS before turning on the car. Anyone can drive, but only the wise driver takes time to find the best route toward the destination. They avoid the traffic, road closures, and roadblocks.

If your goal is to graduate with a master's degree in six years, you cannot waste time chipping away at credit hours from semester to semester. Time is too precious. Life is too unpredictable. The classes you take must directly correlate to your intended major. The activities you partake in must line up with the value system of your master's program. The people you associate with should be like-minded in pursuing similar goals. These simple Power Steps will propel you laps ahead of those simply taking Baby Steps. The goal of Power Steps is to optimize your opportunities to cross the starting line and reach the finish line.

The Mosquito Mindset

Many people who try to start a business begin with only the idea, a sprinkle of hope, and a few bucks. Or if they're looking for a significant other, they have only a good heart and a vision for the future to offer. Even when deciding to go back to school, a slight knowledge of the subject might be all they have. That may seem like too little. But truthfully, that is all you need to get started. Do not be discouraged by what you don't have. Instead, be encouraged by what you do have. Many people have started from a lower position and reached the heights you are aiming for, while even more people have started from a higher position and not made it anywhere near the level you have reached. Your greatest advantage is that you are you and not somebody else. With the little you have,

success is within your grasp.

The Dalai Lama famously said, "If you think you are too small to make a difference, try sleeping with a mosquito."[87] According to *National Geographic*, the average mosquito weighs 0.000088 oz.[88] According to *Live Science*, the average human weighs 136 pounds.[89] One pound equals 16 ounces, so the average human weighs 2176 ounces. That means that for a mosquito to challenge the average person in terms of weight and size, there would have to be approximately 25,727,272 mosquitos. This begs the question: Despite a mosquito being smaller in size than a human, why does the mosquito risk its life to suck blood from humans?

According to Prairie Research Institute, "Only female mosquitoes take blood. They use the protein and iron found in blood to make their eggs. Females feed on nectar and water, as males do."[90] I was surprised to learn that mosquitos do not suck blood for their own survival but rather for ingredients necessary to lay eggs. This means that the mosquito values the lives of future generations over its own survival. That is the mosquito mindset.

Never devalue the significance that your crossing the starting line will have on future generations. Upon releasing my first book, *Powerful Presenting: How to Overcome One of the Nation's Greatest Fears*, a friend of mine named Andie purchased the book. At the time, she was a student at FIU and also teaching elementary students. One day she brought the book to the classroom, and a young girl picked it up and started reading it. She liked what she read and brought it to

Andie to speak about it. Andie began to tell the young girl that she was friends with me. Then the young girl turned the book to look at the cover and saw my face and noticed my name is Jefferson Noel. At the sight of my last name, she erupted with joy: "Noel? That's his last name? That means he must be Haitian!" The girl's exuberant disbelief sprang from the realization that someone my age who has the same background as her had produced that book.

While writing that book, I did not have the young girl's age group in mind as my potential audience, but yet she benefited from the sacrifice. Once you cross the starting line, there is no true measurement for understanding your impact on future generations. The Nobel Peace Prize winner George Bernard Shaw wrote:

> *This is the true joy in life: Being used for a purpose recognized by yourself as a mighty one, being a force of nature instead of a feverish, selfish little clod of ailments and grievances, complaining that the world will not devote itself to making you happy. I am of the opinion that my life belongs to the whole community and as long as I live, it is my privilege to do for it what I can. It is a sort of splendid torch which I have got hold of for the moment and I want to make it burn as brightly as possible before handing it on to future generations.*[91]

> *Once you cross the starting line, there is no true measurement for understanding your impact on future generations.*

Risk is the Currency of Success

Have you ever wondered why many people remain in a toxic relationship that appears to be emotionally and physically draining? Or why nearly four in ten have never left the place in which they were born (according to a Pew Social & Demographic Trends survey)? Have you thought about why people stay friends with someone although they clearly have grown apart?

Part of the reason is what psychologists call status quo bias. Kendra Cherry, author of *The Everything Psychology Book: Explore the Human Psyche and Understand Why We Do the Things We Do* (2nd edition), wrote, "Status quo bias is one type of cognitive bias that involves people preferring that things stay as they are or that the current state of affairs remains the same."[92] She went on to say, "When changes do occur, people tend to perceive them as a loss or detriment."[93]

As the old adage says, "It is better to be with the devil you are familiar with than a strange devil." We are wired to fear losing what we have. Yet we have a conflicting desire to gain what we want. However, that fear to lose causes psychological dehydration of the joy of gaining. That unwelcomed sense of loss causes many people to remain in a state of inaction in an attempt to avoid losing time, energy, resources, relationships, and so forth. However, as an *actiophil*, you must rebel against your natural inclination to settle. Here is the reason: Whether you decide to start or not, safety does not exist. Many people fear beginning because they do not want to leave their comfort zone. They are "content" where they are because the possibility of being somewhere unfamiliar is scary. They are like the child terrified to move into a new neighborhood because that entails attending a new school and making new friends. The child believes the gain of new friends will severely lack compared to the loss of old friends.

In December 2013, I too arrived at the crossroads of the joy of gaining vs. the pain of losing. At that point, societal bliss had wrapped itself comfortably around me. My life resembled a granted wish from blowing a birthday candle. I owned my own car, unlike most of my friends at the time; I had excellent, loving parents who kept a roof over my head and food on my table; and I worked at The Juice Spot, which was owned by Savannah James, LeBron James's wife. I was in a good place in life. I was comfortable. Which was good, until it became bad. My comfort led to stagnancy. My life carried a stench of purposeless apathy.

> As an actiophil, you must rebel against your natural inclination to settle. Here is the reason:
> Whether you decide to start or not, **safety does not exist.**

Once I realized that fact, I was faced with a decision. Either I could do nothing and remain comfortable or I could disrupt the calm rivers in my life by intentionally plunging into a storm of risk. I chose the latter. As an *actiophil*, I knew that whatever decision I made, I would need to be certain that would be the best plan moving forward. Crossing the starting line always involve risk.

During that same month, I decided one evening that I was going to move out of my parents' house to live on my own in Orlando. At the time, I didn't know when and I didn't know how; all I knew was why. And I felt the purpose for transitioning outweighed the risk. I understood that by making this move, I would have to resign from working at the Juice Spot. I would have to forfeit seeing Lebron James almost every day and getting paid a good amount. I would no longer be living with my parents, which would mean I would stop living rent free, my mom's excellent cooking would no longer be accessible, I would be leaving a strong base of friends, and I would have to live in a city I had never known. That was a major starting line to cross. But I decided to move forward anyway.

These same risks are also the ones you will have to face as an *actiophil*. Regardless of which starting line you are crossing and why, you will risk looking foolish, being embarrassed, losing money, losing friends, losing your happiness, losing comfortability, seeming crazy, wasting time.

These risks are not inevitable. But they are a possibility. The possibility of loss is interwoven into the DNA of success. In the same breath, the guarantee of failure is interlaced into complacency. Remaining in a "comfortable" place has the illusion of happiness. Scores of people fall for this delusion and set up camp in front of the starting line. Do not let that be you. *Great reward is born out of great risk.*

Why Matters Most

Some people who have too many resources to count choose not to cross the starting line, while others whose reservoir is nearly dry live in a mental state of GO. Crossing the starting line is mostly about "Why you are starting?" as opposed to "What do you have to start?" There is no one-size-fits all formula to achieve the "sacred bliss" to start. Your why matters more than anything else.

In 2011, Wanda Time created L'union Suite, a Haitian-American lifestyle, tourism, culture, society, and entertainment blog site, created to change the world's perception of Haiti. She uses the platform to spread an authentic visual of Haiti. Wanda wants the next generation to be inspired and join the conversation on improving the country and highlighting the people's God-given talents. To this day, L'union Suite attracts over 10 million visitors a week from all over the world with over 300,000 subscribers via Facebook, Instagram, Tumblr, and Twitter.[94] Wanda's why the linchpin that holds L'union Suite together is. She uses her love for the culture and her educational background to service the Haitian-American community. Wanda's why brought L'union Suite to the apex of the Haitian-American community.

The motivational speaker and best-selling author, Les Brown, often tells the story of the Chinese Bamboo Tree. This tree is unique among its kind because its growth largely depends on the patience and dedication of the planter. When you plant the seed of the Chinese Bamboo Tree in the ground, you must water and fertilize the seed every day. Unfortunately, you will not see immediate results because the Bamboo Tree does not break ground for five years. This means that someone can water and fertilize this seed for 1,825 days straight and be in the dark about whether their methods for growing the tree are working. In the fifth year, something magical happens. The seed produces a visible sign of growth by breaking through the ground. Within six weeks, the Chinese Bamboo Tree grows to an extraordinary ninety feet tall![95]

That is incredible. The Chinese Bamboo Tree teaches us that not all effort will be awarded immediately, but that does not give you permission to lose hope. Your why will bring you to the starting line even if what, when, and how stand in the way of your success. Your why will also sustain your motivation to keep fertilizing and watering. Even if you do not see results in year one. Keep watering and fertilizing. Year two will come, with no sign of progress. Year three will come, and it will seems like you are wasting your energy and resources. Keep watering and fertilizing. Year will come, and the ground will remain flat as the first year. Keep watering and fertilizing; your six-week sprout shall soon come.

Do not put the weight of your decisions on things that do not contribute to your core self. When your actions are why oriented, you will be more determined to work toward the finish line. Stay faithful to your why.

The January 1 Effect

As humans, we put a strong emphasis on dates and symbols. January 1 is the most important day of the year for many people to start. Local gyms experience an exponential increase in membership due to New Year fitness goals. Books fly off the shelves and go out of stock because masses of people decide to read a book a month. Candy stores and bakeries sales fluctuate because people are changing their diet. This happens because we glorify the start of the New Year as the impetus to cross the starting line.

> *Stay faithful to your why.*

I am not opposed to the action that takes place on January 1, but I am vehemently against the inaction that takes place on December 31. The same capability you have to start afresh on

January 1 is the same ability you have to begin your journey on December 31. But instead, we wait. We salivate in eager anticipation for the clock to strike midnight to take the first step. This is what I call the January 1 effect. Our desire to find a symbolic starting point causes us to rationalize stagnancy. It becomes socially acceptable to stand with our mouth open until something happens. Unfortunately, this doesn't only occur at the start of the New Year, but the January 1 Effect works year-round. You may say, I will become a better wife when February 14th comes. I will start going to church consistently starting Easter Sunday. I'm going to become a better father when my child gets better grades. I'm going to run for political office when I secure an endorsement from a large organization. I'm going to go back to school once my child gets born.

> *January 1 has delayed and destroyed more opportunities than it has created.*

The decision to succeed in those areas are great, but the reasoning to kick the can down the road is unnecessary. Unfortunately, we have become creative in finding reasons to wait longer. Let us take the first example. If the wife says she is going to wait until Valentine's Day to treat her husband better. On February 13th, she an say, "Well, let me wait until April 9th. That is his birthday and since that day is all about him, it will be more genuine." Then April 8th comes around. "Well, let me wait until June 29th because that is the day of our wedding anniversary. That day symbolizes love and it will be more intimate and real." Then June 28th comes around and she will find a fresh excuse to not start. That is the problem with the January 1 mindset. So I say this to you:

If you have the ability, resources, and knowledge to start now, then start! If you have the money to purchase healthier foods on December 14th, then do not stuff your face with junk food for 16 more days until January 1. Do not drag your feet until the third Thursday of November to reinvigorate your relationship with your family. Pick up the phone now and start rebuilding your relationship. If you a Christian and feel you are drifting from the faith, do not stall until Easter Sunday to poke your head back into the church.

Mellody Hobson, President of Ariel Investments, in TEDx asked the question, "What is wrong with now?... We've admired the problem long enough. It is time to do something about it."[96] There will always be a reason to stand still and do nothing. Our imagined future will always look better than our present. But the fact is, the future does not exist yet. A minor problem that seemingly prevents you from starting today can easily become a major difficulty tomorrow.

January 1 has delayed and destroyed more opportunities than it has created. You can start any day. Would you rather start a YouTube channel on a unique day like October 17 or wait until January 1 when thousands of other people are encouraging their friends to like and share their new video?

The former is clearly the better option. Stop waiting around. GO!

Forty is Not Always Greater Than Ten

Most of us have been through the phase where we had an idea and we knew that we needed someone to move forward with. I receive those calls all the time. It usually goes as follows:

Person: "Hey Jeff! I haven't heard from you in a while. How are you?"

Jeff: "I am doing well. Life has been interesting for me thus far."

Person: "I see all the great things you are doing in the community with Barbershop Speaks and your new book, being featured all over television and all of that. How is all of that going?"

Jeff: "At times it can be hard to balance everything at once, but I am dedicated to anything I put my time into. But enough about me, what's been good with you?"

Person: "I am doing well, man. I am doing well. I actually have something I am working on right now."

Jeff: "Oh cool, tell me about it."

Person: "Well…[insert their idea]"

Jeff: "Okay. This idea sounds tenable."
Person: "Yeah, but here is the thing. I can't do this by myself. I don't have the time or the experience to get this done."

Jeff: "I understand what you mean."

Person: "Yeah, that's why I am calling you. I see what you are doing with Barbershop Speaks and your book and everything else, and I know you would be a great addition to my team."

Jeff: "Well…thank you. I do think you have a viable idea, and it definitely has potential to go places."

Person: "So what do you think? Are you able to join me?"

Jeff: "Well…as you know, I am already heavily involved in a lot with everything I am doing."

Person: "I understand. I understand. That is why I was hesitant to ask you, but I figured you would be the perfect person to get this off the ground."

Jeff: "I see where you are coming from, my friend. Please give me some time to learn more about what you want to do, and I will let you know how I can help."

Person: "That's great!"

Jeff: "Well…hold on there. If I'm able to put in some time, it would be about ten hours a week max…"

Person: "Ten hours? Man, that's tough. I need someone who is dedicated and committed to this. Maybe this is not the right thing for you. Let me know when you have more time to help. My door will always be open."

Jeff: "I appreciate it, my friend. And regardless if you find someone, lay a foundation down to put yourself in the best position to succeed."

Person: "I will. Thank you for taking my call."

Jeff: "No problem. Thanks for calling me. We will speak soon."

Person: "No doubt. Bye."

Jeff: "Peace out."

Here is the lesson: More likely than not, the person too busy to fully invest in your business is the one who can bring the most value. Finding time from an expert is difficult. Let's say you want to learn how to become a better actor. In a stroke of good fortune, you come across Denzel Washington. You have a short discussion and express your desire to begin acting. He asks you if you need help learning. You reply and say you would like a full-time coach. He is willing to help but can only train you for ten hours a month. Would you turn him down? Probably not. You understand that the value Denzel Washington would give you in ten hours outweighs the forty hours from a regular acting instructor. There is power in experts.

See graph below:

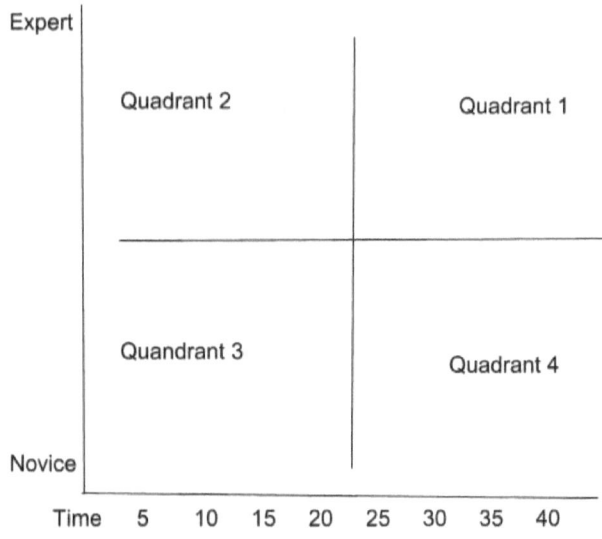

Quadrant 1: When crossing the starting line, if you find someone to join you with ample time and expertise such as in Quadrant 1, that is the absolute ideal. This person understands the journey, has been through the struggle, faced failure, and certainly succeeded. Plus, they are willing to dedicate a large portion of their time to your success. This is Bill Gates teaching you how to code or Anthony Robbins giving you speech lessons full time. Although that would be a blessing of high magnitude, the likelihood of that scenario is extremely low.

Quadrant 2: This is the more realistic scenario. Experts are usually dedicating their time to doing what made them an expert. Therefore, it is understandable why the "ideal" person to join you on the journey cannot allocate a lot of time. But that is okay. As you cross the starting line, guidance from others is necessary, but that guidance shouldn't be the exact replica of a GPS telling you every move you need to make. It is important to keep your journey unique. Leave room for self-discovery. But when necessary, follow a guiding hand that leads toward the finish line.

When someone from Quadrant 2 finds windows in their calendar to help you, take advantage of that blessing. Part of the reason I am constantly in an opportune position to succeed is because I recognize how to maneuver my relationships with experts; I am appreciative of their time and implement their counsel. Saif Ishoof, Vice President of Engagement at FIU, is one of my Quadrant 2 mentors. I receive more value from a one-hour conversation with him than twenty hours with most other people. Every conversation we have produces gold. Remember, forty is not always greater than ten.

Quadrant 3: This situation is not desirable. A non-expert with little time will yield low fruit for your journey.

Quadrant 4: This is someone you can grow with. Through consistency, this person will eventually reach Quadrant 2 level. As the Bible says in the book of Zechariah 4, "Do not despise small beginnings..."[97] The previous section spoke to the importance of compeers in your Dynamic Diamond. Quadrant 4 are your compeers—people willing to run with you, struggle with you, fail with you, then eventually succeed with you.

Playoff Mode

Lebron James has been a dominant force in basketball since the year he was drafted in 2003. From the game he scored his first points to this day, his influence and impact on the game has expanded exponentially. Lebron is known as the greatest basketball player of this generation, and many (including myself) argue he is the greatest NBA player of all time. To put his greatness in perspective, look at these accomplishments:

Awards and honors

- Three-time NBA Champion: 2012, 2013, 2016
- Three-time NBA Finals MVP: 2012, 2013, 2016
- Four-time NBA Most Valuable Player: 2009, 2010, 2012, 2013

- 13-time NBA All-Star: 2005, 2006, 2007, 2008, 2009, 2010, 2011, 2012, 2013, 2014, 2015, 2016, 2017
- Two-time NBA All-Star Game MVP: 2006, 2008
- 11-time All-NBA First Team: 2006, 2008, 2009, 2010, 2011, 2012, 2013, 2014, 2015, 2016, 2017
- Two-time All-NBA Second Team: 2005, 2007
- Five-time NBA All-Defensive First Team: 2009, 2010, 2011, 2012, 2013
- NBA All-Defensive Second Team: 2014
- 2004 NBA Rookie of the Year
- 2004 NBA All-Rookie First Team
- 2008 NBA Scoring Champion
- Two-time Olympic Gold Medal winner: 2008, 2012
- 2004 Olympic Bronze Medal winner
- 2006 FIBA World Championship Bronze Medal winner
- 2007 FIBA Americas Championship Gold Medal winner
- 2012 USA Basketball Male Athlete of the Year
- Commemorative banner in Miami's American Airlines Arena (for his 2012 gold medal won as a member of the Miami Heat)[98]

If you skipped over all these amazing accomplishments, I understand. His accolades are exhausting to read through. After winning a playoff game against the Atlanta Hawks to make it to the NBA finals, LeBron shared one of his favorite quotes by Theodore Roosevelt called "Man in the Arena":

> *It is not the critic who counts; not the man who points out how the strong man stumbles, or where the doer of deeds could have done them better. The credit belongs to the man who is actually in the arena, whose face is marred by dust and sweat and blood; who strives valiantly; who errs, who comes short again and again, because there is no effort without error and shortcoming; but who does actually strive to do the deeds; who knows great enthusiasms, the great devotions; who spends himself in a worthy cause; who at the best knows in the end the triumph of high achievement, and who at the worst, if he fails, at least fails while daring greatly, so that his place shall never be with those cold and timid souls who neither know victory nor defeat.*[99]

LeBron has been the Man in the Arena since his days as a high school player when he was dubbed best player in the country. The reason he has consistently carried the title of most influential basketball player in the world is because of his commitment to remain in playoff mode all year. Including the off season. While many players shut off over the long NBA break, Lebron James is adding new skills to his game. He studies videos of himself from the previous season and sees how he can improve for the coming year. He factors his age into account. He researches what skills he needs to compliment the team as a whole. LeBron dedicates himself to constant improvement because he understands it is only the Man in the Arena who will be criticized. Not the person on the bench or the fans in the bleachers.

> *Self-discovery is the ultimate key to self-mastery.*

The playoff mindset has led LeBron James to eight consecutive NBA Finals. Many people became numb to this streak of greatness because they were accustomed to watching him in the NBA Finals. Lebron is making something that is remarkable look ordinary. He has changed the way we view basketball. He set the bar so high that the criteria to be considered "great" had to be adjusted.

When you are an *actiophil*, breaking past the starting line is not enough. You must run with a passion. Run with meaning. Do not look to see how fast others are going to determine your own pace. Like Lebron James, you need to stay in playoff mode. It's important to remain in a constant state of education. Self-discovery is the ultimate key to self-mastery. Examine yourself to see how you can improve. Don't get comfortable playing preseason games. Get in playoff mode and remain in that state!

Big is Not Always Greater Than Small

We all have big plans and big dreams we would like to see accomplished. Whenever I have a goal in mind, my instincts are to go directly to the peak of the mountain. That mindset is not toxic, but it is not optimal either. When I conceived of Barbershop Speaks, my plan was to grow exponentially within an extremely short period of time. Below are actual goals I set for myself:

- July 2016 - Grand Opening of Barbershop Speaks (expand into two Barber Shops)
- August 2016 - Three barber shops in Miami, one in Orlando

- November 2016 - Five barber shops in Miami, three in Orlando
- January 2017 - Ten barber shops in Miami, five in Orlando, one in Atlanta, one in Tampa
- July 2017 - Fifteen barber shops in Miami, ten in Orlando, five in Atlanta, five in Tampa
- December 2017 - Twenty barber shops in Miami, fifteen in Orlando, ten in Atlanta five in Tampa, three in Chicago
- January 2017 - Twenty barber shops in Miami, fifteen in Orlando, ten in Atlanta, five in Tampa three in Chicago, one in Boston, one in Washington D.C., one in New York

Please keep in mind that I thought these were realistic expectations I had set for myself. Here are the actual results:

- July 2016 - Grand Opening of Barbershop Speaks
- August 2016 - Two barber shops in Miami
- November 2016 - Four barber shops in Miami
- January 2017 - Four Barber shops in Miami
- July 2017 - Four barber shops in Miami
- December 2017 - Four barber shops in Miami
- January 2018 - Four barber shops in Miami
- July 2018 - Four barber shops in Miami and one in Broward

As you can clearly see, I failed horribly in achieving the goals I set for myself. Yet, Barbershop Speaks has been a massive success. I came to realize I did not have the capacity or resources to host consistent events in multiple places at once. Achieving those previously set goals would have inhibited me from achieving in other areas of my life that required my time and energy.

In August 2016, I started as a student at Florida International University. Instead of going the normal route of taking twelve credits, I opted for fifteen credits (five classes) instead. Those classes included Business Communication, Interpersonal/Interracial communication, and Nonverbal Communication. You can imagine how much time school alone demanded of me. In addition, I began working full time as a valet/bell attendant at the Miami Sheraton Hotel and Executive Suites. I was also at the tail end of writing my first book which called for tons of time. And I spoke often at high schools and colleges and events through my community. Managing that type of lifestyle while Directing Barbershop Speaks in multiple cities, plenty of barber shops, and coordinating event times and attendees would have been hectic. Even if I delegated a majority of the tasks, *becoming too big would have shrunk my chances of success.* I found that big is not always greater than small.

Here's another practical example of this truism: Imagine you are the owner of a shampoo company. Through efforts of marketing, customer acquisition strategies, plus more, let's say you sell only forty bottles of shampoo a week. That may not be ideal for the business to sustain itself over a long period, but it is reasonable given the level of output that can be produced effectively. Realistically, however, you would want the business to grow.

Then, to your good fortune, a lice epidemic breaks out in the country. Now, thousands of people in your market segment are scrambling to purchase shampoo bottles, and the demand is for you to produce and sell two thousand bottles a week. This may seem good for the business because of the increase in demand for your product. However, *this rose that life handed you is plagued with thorns.* Going from forty shampoo bottles a week to two thousand requires significantly more staff to manufacture the bottles. Then, you will need the capacity to handle customers' requests and complaints. The methods you use to distribute the bottles to customers must be expedited as a result of the high demand. Not to mention, each new hire must be trained to maintain the quality of your products and customer service. Getting all of that done within a short time frame is nearly impossible.

This outbreak in lice would actually cause a breakdown of your business. The products would be poor quality given the new, inexperienced employees. The shipping of the products would inevitably be delayed, which would bring a myriad of complaints that would go unanswered. People would demand refunds. By the time the lice outbreak was over, hundreds of people would still be waiting for their bottle of shampoo, and many more would be demanding their money back (maybe even lawsuits). Your customer reviews on Yelp, Facebook, Amazon, and the like would be deplorable. All because you became too big, too fast.

Dear *actiophil*, big is not always greater than small. You need to be prudent. Maybe asking your girlfriend to marry you within three weeks of dating is far too early. Maybe taking fifteen credits instead of nine is too much. Or even trying to purchase a $2,000 camera for your YouTube Channel is too soon. There are ways to work toward your finish line, but do not jeopardize the joy of a promising future because you feel you are going too slow. In other words: **Do not feed steak to a baby.**

When to Say *NO* and Know When to *GO*

Nothing magical happens when a decision is made. If you decide to pursue becoming an NFL player, the ramifications of that decision include giving up a lot of leisure time, going to multiple practices a day, working out endlessly, maintaining good grades, dieting properly, creating a certain public persona, and so on. Saying yes to one thing requires you to simultaneously say yes to thousands of other options. At the same, you also say an astounding NO to millions of other possible decisions. Saying yes to cross the starting line is never an isolated decision.

During my first semester as an undergraduate at FIU, I knew the importance of getting involved. Prior to enrolling at FIU, I served in the student government at Valencia College. Being FIU was a different institution, I went to the student government's office to inquire about the responsibilities and expectations for a position. After they explained everything in detail, I took some time to decide, then responded with "No. I will not apply." Although I desired to get involved, that "no" was the right decision at that time. My life was already packed full of commitments at that time.

A full year later, in 2017, I went back to inquire about joining the student government at FIU. This time, after reviewing a full overview of the position of Senator of Communications and Journalism, I said yes. This time, I was ready to sprint. This decision to GO one year later was healthy. My life had a lot less clutter, and I was more focused and prepared. *I crossed the starting line at **my** ideal moment.*

GO vs NO

There is no universal formula to teach you the precise moment when to cross, but there are indicators you should strongly consider before making a decision. These signs are guideposts that will lead you to toward the best route:

GO	NO
You are mentally sound	You feel mentally depleted
Ready to invest emotional energy	You are emotionally distant

You have strong support	You are completely isolated
You are willing to learn	You think you know everything
You embrace the possibility of failure	You feel failure is the end
You are willing to take risk	You think everything will work out perfectly
Your actions will align with your values	You will have to compromise your values
You are passionate	You are apathetic
You feel challenged	Everything will be easy

Many people hesitate at the starting line not because of research or because they analyzed the pros and cons but because of the one-inch wall referred to earlier. If you fit the mold of the former category, then strategize when the best time is to make your move. Once you decide to move, do not look back. *The beauty of the future will shine brighter than the beauty of the past.* I have more control in my life because I know what I want. I also understand what I do not need.

Section 3

Never Cross the Starting Line With

Throughout this book, I have emphasized the importance of crossing the starting line. Your future success hinges on whether or not you will GO. Standing frozen like a statue is not an ideal way to live. Once you decide to cross the starting line, an examination of yourself is crucial. You may discover lurking thoughts and/or experiences that hinder success. These can include a scarcity mentality, open wounds, an empty roadmap, and unbearable baggage. This is how to overcome such things:

The Scarcity Mentality

During my elementary school years, the school held a field day every year. Students from every grade level always looked forward to this day because it showcased the best talent in our class. Sixth grade marked the final field day in our elementary careers, which also made it the most competitive field day. The races—one-mile runs, sprints, and relays—brought the most excitement. My sixth-grade field day was especially competitive because the teachers split all of us students into four different "homerooms." Although I desperately wanted to compete with my homeroom, my classmates never chose me to race in those competitions. The reason? I ran too slow. But I and all the other slow runners still cheered our team on with joy. On field day, we all coveted the top spot. If we received first place, that meant the others teams would have receive second, third, and fourth places. Our victory would become their defeat.

> *If you have a scarcity mindset, please do not take it with you past the starting line. You will damage more people on the pathway to your own destruction.*

However, this did not hold true in the classroom. In math, history, or science class, the highest grade was an A. But if the person next to me managed an A, that did not mean the highest I can earn would be a B. My grade was not based on the actions of the people around me. That is the same in life; there can be two winners. Crossing the starting line is less about securing the number one spot and more about earning an A. Those who are obsessed with winning no matter who gets hurt suffer from what Stephen Covey (219) calls the Scarcity Mentality:

> *Most people are deeply scripted in what I call the Scarcity Mentality, They see life as having only so much, as though there were only one pie out there. And if someone were to get a big piece of the pie, it would mean less for everybody else...People with a Scarcity Mentality have a very difficult time sharing recognition and credit, power or profit—even with those who help in production. They also have a very hard time being genuinely happy for the successes of other people—even, and sometimes especially members of their own family or close friends and associates. It's almost as if something is being taken from them when someone else receives special recognition or windfall gain or has remarkable success or achievement...People with a Scarcity Mentality harbor secret hopes that others might suffer misfortune—not terrible, but acceptable misfortune that would keep them "in their place." They're always comparing, always competing. They give their energies to possessing things or other people in order to increase their worth.*[100]

These words by Stephen Covey pierce the soul. People who have a Scarcity Mentality are not *actiophils*. I do not care how many times they cross the starting line. An *actiophil* is "a genuine person who loves to take action toward a purposeful outcome." The key word here is *genuine*. If you have a scarcity mindset, please do not take it with you past the starting line.

You will damage more people on the pathway to your own destruction.

Open Wounds

I rarely discourage people from crossing the starting line. Only in a few instances. One of which is if you have any open wounds in the area you are working to reach. For example, if you are twenty-four hours removed from a long-term relationship that ended terribly, it may not be a wise decision to immediately dive headfirst into the dating scene. Too many questions remain unanswered and emotions unexamined for you to realistically put yourself in the optimal position. If you ran for an elected position and only garnered 5 percent of the vote, maybe sitting back to obtain a deeper understanding of your constituents and building relationships with them should be your priority.

You must exercise wisdom. Heal from the wounds of failure before you try again. If you cross the starting line too soon without committing to fixing the original problems, you will sabotage your chances of ever reaching success.

My first business, Noel Healthy Living, received all of my eighteen-year-old energy from sunup to sundown every day. Due to the immense pressure I heaped onto myself, coupled with a poor execution plan and other factors, my business failed and closed within four months. That was embarrassing. After that failure, my options narrowed to two: I could start another business or get a job. I chose the latter. Although I wanted to go the business route, I was still recovering from the financial and social blowback of failing. My fresh wounds needed to be treated. Thankfully, I understood that and decided to apply for a job.

One calendar year later, I was in a different position in life and found an opportunity to start another business. This time, I succeeded. I allowed my wounds to heal before I decided to cross the starting line again.

An Empty Roadmap

Those who drive with no destination are always lost. My father was a taxi driver for twenty-three years. He has boatloads of experience driving people to and from places throughout Miami. I'm sure most experiences were good, but the few that were bad are unforgettable. My father would tell me stories of people who call for a taxi but did not know the exact location of their destination. The conversation would go something like this:

Customer: "I would like to go to Hilton Hotel"

Taxi Driver: "Which one?"

Customer: "The Hilton Hotel in Miami."

Taxi Driver: "I know. We are already in Miami. There are many Hiltons in Miami. Do you have the address of the Hilton?"

Customer: "I don't know the exact address. But I know it shouldn't be too far from here."

Taxi Driver: "I need you to be more specific. There is a Hilton in Miami Beach, Downtown, Coconut Grove, on Blue Lagoon Drive, etc."

Customer: "I don't know. Just drive to the nearest one."

You can imagine my dad's frustration as he circled around the city looking for the right Hilton. For that reason, he always asked for the full address when he carted us somewhere. In fact, he refused to turn on the car unless he knew exactly where he was going. If we didn't have the address, we would protest, "Dad, just drive to this area and once we are there, we can tell you exactly where to go." But in our father's wisdom, he would refuse because there would inevitably be a complication such as, "Oh, I thought there was a 7-11 at this corner; the place to turn must be another block down." And once we were in that situation, we would inevitably end up searching for the destination longer than the time we actually spent there.

That is the dilemma you will face if you start the journey without a roadmap. People who know where they are going will always arrive there faster than people who *think* they know where they are going. Even if the unsure person arrives at the destination, they will not know because the final outcome is a mystery. However, the person with a roadmap has a clear measurement of failure and success.

Unbearable Baggage

I am fully convinced that one of the greatest inventions of all time is the airplane. I first ventured onto a plane at the age of nineteen, both terrified and excited. Thankfully, the flight lasted less than forty-five minutes, from Orlando to Miami, Florida. I remember looking out the window in awe of the beauty of the friendly skies and equally amazed at the innovation of humankind to build a device that transport millions of people around the world 30,000 feet in the sky every day. I told myself, *I will never get use to this.* Every time I board a plane, I take a moment to appreciate this invention.

On the other hand, planes don't so enamor me that I lose sight of the cost associated with flying. Especially when transporting luggage. According to the US Department of Transportation, airlines will have made $4.57 billion from checked bag fees in 2017. Surely I contributed to that number.[101] A 2016 Money.com article titled *Best (and Worst) Airline Baggage Fees* reported that "the median fee for your first checked bag is now $25, and $35 for your second checked bag."[102] Here is a graph from Money research to illustrate standard fees for checking bags at the ticket counter for US domestic flights:

Airline	First Checked Bag	Second Checked bag
Spirit	$50	$60
Frontier	$40	$45
Delta	$25	$35
American	$24	$35
United	$25	$35
Hawaii	$25	$35
JetBlue	$25	$35
Sun Country	$25	$35
Alaska	$25	$25
Southwest	$0	$0

Last updated 3/15/2016. Source: MONEY research.[103]

Notice how the price of the second checked bag is usually more expensive than the cost of the first checked bag. The more bags you carry, the more you pay (with the exception of Southwest, who does not charge at all). For the airlines, checked baggage is a big revenue source. For the consumer, this drains the wallet. Too much baggage will hurt your wallet on a plane. In the same way, too much baggage will hurt your progress on a journey.

Crossing the starting line with a lot of baggage can and will cost you more than money. You can risk damaging your mental and emotional health. Friendships can suffer and business relationships can be severed. The less baggage you carry past the starting line, the further you can go. Therefore, I encourage you to proceed as follows:

GO without envy. Go without discouragement. GO without anger. GO without distrust. GO without vengeance. GO without self-doubt. GO without insecurities. GO without shame. GO without depression. GO without guilt. GO without self-hate.

GO, without baggage.

You might find it a struggle to leave every vile and counterproductive emotion or feeling behind. It is possible to cross the starting line, trudge through the journey, and succeed while carrying one or more pieces of baggage but not ideal. Too much baggage can lead to deep distress and long-term negative consequences. Never cross the starting line with excessive baggage. The cost is too great.

Lines to Never Cross

At this point in the book, I'm sure you are eager to cross the starting line. You made up your mind to begin learning that musical instrument. Or maybe the Commissioner seat in your municipality is open and you resolved to run for that position. I am well pleased that you are ready. However, I want you to keep in mind that not every line should be crossed. Some situations says "DO NOT ENTER" on it and you should listen. I will be irresponsible if I encourage you to cross the starting line at the expense of your own interest or the well-being of others. Some lines, under any circumstances, should never be crossed.

Line of Values

I am a proponent of filtering decisions and actions through one's value system. Our actions stem from our values and innermost beliefs. Our lives are centered around what we feel is best for ourselves and those around us, based on what we prioritize. For example, if I am a teenager who values physical training over academics, if provided the option, I would likely go to the gym after school to work out as opposed to tutoring. If my top priority is strengthening friendships, there is a strong possibility I will attend my best friend's birthday party as opposed to attending a football game with work colleagues. Our values drive our decisions.

However, there are times in our life when we lose sight of the end goal and become entrenched in the journey. Linda and Charlie Bloom, authors of *Secrets of Great Marriages: Real Truths from Real Couples about Lasting Love*, speak about the dangers of Corporate Marriage Syndrome. That term may not be widely used, but is definitely widely practiced. "Corporate Marriage Syndrome occurs when the company requires allegiance to the corporation over and above the employee's time and energy devoted to family."[104] Does that sound familiar? Of course, it does. This country is rife with people who are more keen to please their boss than their spouse.

Linda and Charlie Bloom tell the story of Regan and Lucia. Regan took a corporate job when his youngest child was eighteen months old and the two other children were four and seven. The high demand of Regan's job led Lucia to feel she was a single mother raising their three children, which in turn stressed the couple's marriage:

> *The twelve years before Regan took the corporate job had been largely harmonious. That harmony was shattered by the corporation's overpowering needs. Lucia and Regan had differences before he was a corporate man, which they had worked out amicably. But during this time, the irreconcilable difference kept them both in a chronic state of irritability. Lucia's stance was "I want you to leave this job. It's causing great harm to you, me and our children." Regan's stance was, "I love my job and I'm not giving it up."*
>
> *Lucia began referring to her husband's career as the "mistress." She felt that Regan loved her more than he loved her, because he spent more time with her. She felt that his job was an enemy she couldn't fight, so she waited for him to finally came back into the family. Lucia told me that for most of the time, she wasn't sure that she could stay strong enough to last the ordeal. It was a long five years.*[105]

Thankfully, Regan eventually realized the error in his attitude. He awakened to the reality that his work life was placing a burden too great to bear on his family. Lucia was painfully suffering while Regan unknowingly (or stubbornly) caused that pain. After Regan decided, then acted, on getting back to his values, he said, "We gladly made these sacrifices, and what we gained in exchange for letting go of the material well-being was an emotional, psychological, and spiritual well-being that was well worth the tradeoff. Our life as a family after extricating ourselves from the corporate world was immeasurably enhanced. It was a close call, but we made it through, wiser than before about what really matters."

Regan crossed the line of values. His family life suffered as a result. His children experienced at least five years without an involved father. His wife endured at least five years without her husband placing her at the center of his world. If Regan had never returned to the source of his values, we don't know how deep he would have dug into the depths of familial isolation.

As you prepare to cross the starting line, be sure to never cross your line of values. You do not want to be Regan. He became so caught up in reaching the finish line of his career that he neglected to nurture the journey he started many years prior. Dealing with someone who is abandoning their values may be difficult. However, working to prevent yourself from steering away from your own values is within your power.

This is how to ensure you never cross the line of values:

Live a Life of Self-examination

Job interviews are nerve-racking. I remember applying for my first job as a valet attendant. Fear ran concurrently with my blood throughout my body. After learning I was invited to do the interview, I was also informed it would be with a group. I remember telling myself, *Not only will I embarrass myself in front of the employer, but I will be put to shame in front of the more polished and experienced candidates.* After careful review of such fear arose within me, I discovered that most of my trepidation stemmed from the employer asking a question that would expose my ignorance about my own behavior and myself.

This led me to a realization: I must interview myself before others interview me. There must be a period of self-evaluation; you must place yourself underneath the microscope, then examine the fine details of who you are, what you value, and how you live out those values.

Accompanying yourself through a period of self-examination is good, not only for job interviews but also for shining a light in the dark corners of your world that would otherwise be unknown to you. Here is a rule to live by: *Never allow someone to ask you something you never asked yourself.* Once you find those values, never cross that line.

> *You must place yourself underneath the microscope, then examine the fine details of who you are, what you value, and how you live out those values.*

Line of Integrity

Being a person of integrity can be a challenge. In a world where fulfillment is hard to grasp and easy to lose, expediency is extremely tempting. Corners that were once necessary to maneuver around may begin to look like a roadblock that should be removed. Lack of integrity has shriveled many people down to a symbol of shame. The Nixon presidency led to a dumpster fire of disgrace because of mountains of lies, spying on political opponents, and crimes committed at his request. Too many marriages have ended in disastrous divorces out of infidelity. College students are expelled every year because of plagiarism and cheating. The list can continue about folks who crossed not only the starting line but also the line of integrity.

Manage Train Learn (MTL) share a compelling story about integrity called "The New Emperor":

> An ageing emperor in the East decided on a novel way to choose his successor. He called the city's youths to his palace. Handing out some special seeds, he told them, "Go and plant these seeds. In a year's time, I will judge your plants and choose the new emperor." One boy named Ling took his pot home and planted the seed. Every day he watered it but nothing grew. Even though his friends at school were talking about their growing plants, Ling only had an empty pot.
>
> When the day came to return to the palace, Ling went with a frightened heart. The emperor appeared. All the other youths had magnificent plants. When the emperor saw Ling's plant, he summoned him to the front and announced to the crowd, "Behold your new emperor! He has courage and integrity for all the seeds I gave you were boiled and useless. He was the only one not to cheat. He will be a wise ruler over you all."[106]

You will face similar temptations to backslide—scenarios that challenge your bond with integrity. But that line should never be crossed. Let the world masquerade with their fake plants while you stand boldly with a good conscious. *The long-term reward for integrity will always supersede the short-term benefits of deceit.* Cross the starting line with honesty.

As an *actiophil*, part of your duty is to love taking action without stepping on anyone's necks to get to the top.

Line of Conformity

You have a plan. You have a vision. You want to succeed.
BUT.
No one is paying attention to you. No one is giving you their time. No one is helping.
What do you do next?
Here are a couple of options:

- Stop your plan dead in its tracks.
- Manipulate others to help.
- Conform your plan to please others.
- Adjust your plan to make it better.

The first option is a non-starter. Unless crossing the starting line will plunge your family into unrecoverable debt or break apart the fabric of society, you should not stop your plan. Similar to promises, plans are not made to be broken. That throws option one out the window. As an *actiophil*, part of your duty is to love taking action without stepping on anyone's necks to get to the top. That removes option number two. Thus, you are left with options three and four—conform your plan to please others or adjust your plan to make it better.

The former will make you average. The latter will make you great.

To understand which option is best, please understand there is a stark difference between adjusting and conforming; those words/actions are not synonymous. To conform is to abandon one's set of values to appeal to a lower standard, while adjusting is to re-examine then restructure one's plan toward a singular goal. *If the line of conformity is crossed, you put yourself in the backseat of your own vehicle, while placing society in the driver's seat.* Once you lose decision-making ability over your own journey, society can and will steer you in any direction. Regardless of your best interest. Dear *actiophil*, adjusting is greater than conforming. When crossing the starting line, understand that plans do change but shouldn't be broken. The perfect, bulletproof plan is impossible. There are too many unknown variables. This leaves us with an important question:

Q: How can I adjust without conforming?

A: Fix your plan to better serve your final outcome. Never conform your desired goal to fix your problems.

Look inward before you make change outward. First, ask yourself why you decided to cross the starting line. What was your initial "why"? Your "why" shouldn't change. Determine how to change your methods on the journey without changing the destination. In business, the term "pivot" is often used to describe adjusting. Writer Alan Spoon notes in an INC article that "[pivoting] can be a tool to discover additional growth—growth you might otherwise have overlooked."[107]

Challenge yourself to find blind spots in your thinking. Seek out mentors who have walked the same path as you. Open yourself to the possibility that more resources exist. The goal while adjusting is to grow to be available for new opportunities. Conforming settles for what is already present. Never cross the line of conformity.

Line of Legality

Do not break the law. Look at the people in leadership positions today whose lives have been tarnished by their own doing. Some people are constantly under siege from investigations and lawsuits because of dishonesty and greed. I understand the temptation to reach the finish line faster. But do not cross the starting line at the peril of your freedom.

Line of Pleasure

There are many reasons to cross the starting line. Arguably, the most pressing reason to cross is out of self- interest, happiness, and pleasure. That is not an inherently bad reason. I believe strongly in the need for individuals to love themselves before they love others. To place others before yourself is not feasible, nor is it sustainable. For example, flight attendants always tell you that in an emergency, you should place the oxygen mask on yourself before you put it on children. Living a pleasurable life is interconnected with loving oneself.

On the other hand, too much pleasure is an open invitation to depravity. Debi Acharya, a professional in the field of health safety environment and quality wrote in an article titled "Anything in Excess Is Bad": "If we eat too much, we get stomach ache and digestive problems. Too much of sleep makes us lazy and too much of money steals our peace. The irony is despite knowing that, many of us want more and more."[108]

He goes on to provide examples of the problem of excess.

- Excessive speed results in accident but there are millions who prefer to speed as it thrills them forgetting that it also kills.
- The food will be tasteless but eatable if there is no salt, but if there is excess salt, the food will be tasteless as well as uneatable.
- We need water in a river for our daily living, but if the water is in excess, flood results.
- The government gives us subsidies to combat inflation, but excessive subsidy for many commodities will make the economic system of the country bankrupt.
- Love your children, but excessive love will make you blind to the mistakes of the kids which will ruin them...
- A well-known speaker gets booed by the audience if his speech lingers and exceeds the time limit.[109]

Crossing the line of pleasure is no different from excess salt, the overflow of river water, 100 mph in a school zone, or even a parent being complicit to all decisions of their children. When you are crossing the starting line, your goal should not be pain, but it definitely should not be an overflow of pleasure either. The Christian apologist, best-selling author, and philosopher Ravi Zacharias writes about the problem of pleasure in his book *Can Man Live Without God?*:

> One of the most powerful stories I have ever heard on the nature of the human heart is told by Malcolm Muggeridge. Working as a journalist in India, he left his residence one evening to go to a nearby river for a swim. As he entered the water, across the river he saw an Indian woman from the nearby village who had come to have her bath.
>
> Muggeridge impulsively felt the allurement of the moment, and temptation stormed into his mind. He had lived with this kind of struggle for years but had somehow fought it off in honor of his commitment to his wife, Kitty. On this occasion, however, he wondered if he could cross the line of marital fidelity. He struggled just for a moment and then swam furiously toward the woman, literally trying to outdistance his conscience. His mind fed him the fantasy that stolen waters would be sweet, and he swam the harder for it. Now he was just two or three feet away from her, and as he emerged from the water, any emotion that may have gripped him paled into insignificance when compared with the devastation that shattered him as he looked at her.

"She was old and hideous...and her skin was wrinkled and, worst of all, she was a leper....This creature grinned at me, showing a toothless mask." The experience left Muggeridge trembling and muttering under his breath, "What a dirty lecherous woman!" But then the rude shock of it dawned upon him—it was not the woman who was lecherous; it was his own heart.[110]

As you cross the starting line, examine your motives and your heart. Seek pleasure, not at the expense of your own happiness but to the benefit of your well-being and those around you. In so doing, you will avoid becoming one of the many people depressed because of overload of pleasure.

5 Reasons They Don't Want You to GO

> They say no, not because you cannot but because they don't have the skill set or resources to achieve it themselves.

Unfortunately, many people judge you based on their own expertise and abilities to accomplish feats. Do not ask a mailman for advice to determine how to make rockets 25 percent lighter. Their lack of knowledge will cause them to see your goal as lofty or impossible, whereas a rocket scientist or someone who works at NASA can give you a more level-headed understanding. The mailman may discourage the pursuit of your goal purely out of ignorance on the subject or out of jealousy of your ambition.

Many people will find your success to be a hindrance to their own. They will feel threatened in your presence, causing them to feel the only way to lift themselves up is to bring you down. Think about it. If you and another person are fighting for the same spot but you are more talented than the other person, the only way for them to win is to ensure your talents are hidden and not being used. If they succeed in doing this, your light never shines because it is with doubt. Their light, although it may be dimmer, will shine the brightest because it is not hidden.

Dear *actiophil*, do not fall into such a trap. Never allow someone else's inadequacies to sully your abilities in the marketplace of execution. You possess the ability to GO and leave negative people in your dust. All that matters in the end is: Are you fulfilling your purpose? If the answer to that question is not affirmative, then you are leaving your abilities and talents to spoil like a carton of milk out in the sun.

What are you trying to create? Why haven't you start yet?

Because they have seen you fail plenty of times in the past.

As a serial entrepreneur, creator, and planner, I find it commonplace to have a graveyard of failed ideas or businesses. That is okay. People will judge you based on the defeats in your past and not the hope of your future. Let them judge. The sheer fact that you have started shows your ability and willingness to experience success. These traits are needed to accomplish anything in the first place.

I am a huge advocate for failing fast. I'd rather fail ten times before becoming successful ten years down the road than to never fail and be successful in twenty years. The longer you wait for the perfect time to start, the farther you will have to travel to reach success. Failure serves as a weight room, where each time you fail is a bicep curl or squat. If you keep up the repetition, the result will always be a much stronger and faster version of yourself. Even if others do not see the improved version of yourself, that is fine. The most important person is the man/woman in the mirror. If others do not see your improvement from your previous attempts, your job is not to convince them. Your focus should be crossing the starting line to eventually reach the finish line.

Who are you waiting on to validate your need to start?

The answer should be, "No one!"

> *Never allow someone else's inadequacies to sully your abilities in the marketplace of execution.*

It has never been done.

People are natural doubters. If they have not seen it, then it doesn't exist nor can it come into existence. To convince someone to accept that your vision can come into fruition, you have to be extremely persuasive. At the same time, keep in mind that everyone doesn't need to be convinced. The entire world is not required to believe in you before GO. Having friends and family aboard is helpful, but it can be tedious to earn everyone's approval.

If it has never been done, that is great. You can be the first. Or you can find what is similar that already exists, then create a framework to success from there. Charles H. Duell, commissioner of the US patent office in 1899, is commonly recognized to have said, "Everything that can be invented has been invented."[111] Now, it doesn't take a genius to understand how fallacious and ill-informed that statement was. Especially given that it was said in the late nineteenth century. To name just a few, Top Tenz shared some inventions that changed the world after that statement: nuclear power, the personal computer, the airplane, the automobile, rocketry, the submarine, antibiotics, television, the internet, radio.[112]

What type of world would we live in if the Wright brothers had adopted the mindset of Charles H. Duell? Or if Steve Jobs had shrugged his shoulders and refrained from pushing for the personal computer? What about Henry Ford's intelligence and tenacity to mass-produce the world's first automobile?

All these people decided to cross the starting line despite no precedent for the journey they committed to traveling on. They could have used available excuses, but they chose not to. You should adopt that same mindset.

The world has changed dramatically since Charles H. Duell's statement. Trends are tilting toward rapid innovation and creative-like lifestyles. *The future belongs to those who cross the starting line toward a future the past cannot recognize.* The world has many Charles H. Duells. But there can only be one person to achieve the purpose in your life. That is you. Don't wait. GO!

Your passion for what you say you want done is not clearly seen.

People will not encourage you to put time and energy into something they don't think you believe in. You must value your journey. The old adage says that "walk is greater than talk." I take it a little deeper to say that "talk is meaningless without walk." You must want it. Do not drag anyone into something you do not desire to see completed.

One day, I was at Walmart shopping for some common household items. To my surprise, I ran into a friend whom I have not seen in years. We bantered for about five minutes and reminisced about old times. We agreed to meet up the next week to catch up some more. When we finally met together, it was weird and different from what I expected. He had a different tone and mood. I figured something was wrong, but I did not immediately ask him. As we continued the conversation, he began to make a business pitch. As soon as he began, I felt as though I was at a funeral. Not only was his pitch boring and disinteresting, he did not seem to believe in what he was saying. I was embarrassed for him. There was no passion. No energy. No determination.

Although I believe my friend was able to execute the business, I doubt he was motivated to do it. When you want to cross the starting line, it needs to be done with the vigor and passion of a hungry lion chasing down an obese gazelle. Anything less than that is a waste of my time and yours. In the words of Les Brown, "You gotta be hungry!"[113]

They don't want you to win.

Some people might discourage you from starting because they think you will fail. On the other hand, someone may discourage you from starting because they think you will be successful. The record producer DJ Khaled observed, "They don't want you to win."[114] As an *actiophil*, you must be careful with whom you share your victories. Do not let others downplay your success or remove the joy of victory from your life.

In psychology, there's a concept called Social Comparison Theory. This theory, developed by psychologist Leo Festinger, argues that "individuals determine their own social and personal worth based on how they stack up against others they perceive as somehow faring better or worse."[115] In an attempt for some people to mentally climb the ladder of success, they will first convince themselves and you that you are worse than what reality suggests. When I was serving as president of the student government, a student leader told me he felt my campus was "dead weight." From his perspective, the only way to win was to see me lose, although technically we were playing for the same team. Such are the sad, pernicious effects of those entangled in social comparison.

Do not be discouraged. Never determine whether or not you should start based on the half-baked opinion of insecure people. Recognizing those people in your life is important. DJ Khaled was right when he said, "They don't want you to win." But even more so, they don't want you to start. Be a rebel. GO!

5 Reasons to GO

Action is a necessity to progress.

Every win I ever enjoyed came from hard work I endured. I have been in conversations with people who desired to write a book, but they never finished drafting the words "Chapter 1." From my experience in the world of starting, I find that the first steps toward the finish line set the tone for the entire journey. My thoughts and ideas alone never brought me anything I yearned for. However, when my hands and legs join the action, the chances of me reaching my goal skyrocket from 0 percent to whatever the chances are that I will succeed. Whether 5 percent or 75 percent, it's still a better chance than doing nothing at all.

That is why leaving behind the comfortability of inaction is imperative. Some chance is better than no chance. Moving a couple of steps forward is far better than sitting on your hands. The desire to progress must be married with the passion to take action.

Experience outweighs speculation.

For me as a high school senior, the only thing more nerve-wracking than passing classes for graduation was who I would be taking to prom. That was the big question. At the time, I did not have an affinity for any of the women at my school. However, a young lady at my church was the apple of my eye. I was entranced by her beauty and enamored by her faith in God. Although we lived in two different counties, I desperately wanted to go to prom with her. The only problem was, she didn't know I existed. I am sure she knew my name, but I am also sure I occupied zero space in her thoughts. I was in a dilemma.

I remember trying my best to decode nonverbal gestures to discover if she had noticed me and possibly had mutual feelings. That did not work. As the school year progressed and the deadline to purchase prom tickets crept around the corner, my nervousness rose to unprecedented heights. I remember trying to convince one of my best friends, Junior, that my asking her was not worth it. Then I created a short list of women I could potentially ask who went to my school. After listening to me babble endlessly, Junior said,

"Jeff. You already know who you want to go to prom with. Why are you scared? Why are you making this more complicated than this should be? You know what you want. Go for it!" I decided to listen.

> *I would rather take a break on an upward escalator than on a treadmill.*

That next Wednesday, I saw her at church, and I told myself, "It's all or nothing." When Bible study ended, she headed toward her car in the parking lot, and I made my move. After lines of stuttering and brain farts and freezes, I finally made my ask. Guess what? SHE SAID YES! Overjoyed with excitement as I leaned in for the goodbye/thank you hug, I inadvertently stepped on her foot. Despite the embarrassment, I was still happy because I had put aside senseless speculation and taken action. Even if the answer I was hoping for had not been forthcoming, I'm sure I would have been at peace. I figured it was better to experience what I desired as opposed to speculating on "What if?"

Standing still is akin to moving backwards

Not only does inaction prevent progress but it also promotes digression. Think of it this way: According to the Scientific American publication, "The surface of the earth at the equator moves at a speed of 460 meters per second—or roughly 1,000 miles per hour."[116] Therefore, we are always moving even if we are standing still. Motion is a constant in life.

Life is like a car that can only switch between drive, neutral, and reverse. When you shift to drive, you place yourself in a position to move toward your desired goal. In neutral, you give the control to whomever wants to take advantage of you. In reverse, you lose sight of the finish line.

I would rather take a break on an upward escalator than on a treadmill.

Regardless of who you are and what you do, folk are running at unbelievable speeds toward the same goal you desire. The second you go into neutral, you begin to move backward as though you are on a treadmill. As an *actiophil*, choose drive.

Everything you enjoy today is because someone was unafraid to start yesterday

I am a firm believer that we are living in some of the best times in human history. Not only because of the abundance of knowledge and information at our fingertips (literally) but also because we are the beneficiaries of an inheritance from action-oriented inventors, scientists, philosophers, and more. Technologies from the microwave to the instruments that measure and detect hurricanes significantly improve our quality of life. We enjoy these pleasures because someone sacrificed their time and comfort to ensure the present and future live better.

Whatever good thing you withhold from the world robs future generations. When you live out your passions, it affects more than you: an incalculable domino chain ripples into the lives of many people that you know and millions more that you don't know. In case you didn't realize it already, this is an extraordinary responsibility. If you carry the mindset that your life matters and all you do is impactful, then you will understand the significance in everything you do and all you choose not to do. However, if you are of the school of thought that everything is meaningless and your life is inherently worthless, the logical conclusion would be for you to become lethargic and unproductive.

But everything you do *is* meaningful! Your life is intrinsically worthy. Whether your contribution to this earth is starting a YouTube channel or working in government, your choices are impactful. As the thirty-fourth president of the United States, Dwight D. Eisenhower stated, "The history of free men is never written by chance but by choice—their choice."[117] That truth is an important reason to GO.

Bad Doctor is Still a Doctor

Marshall Goldsmith, an American Leadership Coach, wrote in his book *What Got You Here, Won't Get You There*, "Doctors may be the most delusional. I once told a group of MDs that my extensive research proved that exactly half of all MDs graduated in the bottom half of their medical school class. Two doctors in the room insisted this was impossible."[118] If you don't see the humor in that, I encourage you to read it again. Interestingly enough, doctors who barely made it out of medical school is still a doctor. They can write prescriptions and give expert opinions. And they can certainly diagnose you.

Many people, especially perfectionists, are unwilling to GO unless they are "the best." Honestly, I don't blame them. That is actually part of my philosophy. Dr. Martin Luther King famously said, "If a man is called to be a street sweeper, he should sweep streets even as a Michelangelo painted, or Beethoven composed music or Shakespeare wrote poetry."[119]

However, I encourage you to cross the starting line even if you are not the best. I urge you to start as an average street sweeper. Then grow to become the best. Same as the doctors who graduated at the bottom of their class. Maybe they are not the best or even in the top fifty, but it is better to do something, gain experience, build new connections and grow as opposed to staring at the wall in hopes of becoming an expert on the couch.

Encouraging lackluster exploits is not in my character. However, I will choose to be average over being nothing any day. A bad doctor is still a doctor. And because of practice and studying, the bad doctor can become a good doctor. Maybe even a great doctor. And one day, maybe the best. But that progression will never take place if the doctor never crosses the starting line.

Bonus - You Only Live once (YOLO)

In 2011, the Canadian Rapper Aubrey Graham, better known as Drake, released a song called "The Motto." This song shot up the charts and was nominated for a Grammy for Best Rap Song. Part of what caused an explosion of people loving the song is the expression Drake used in the chorus. That phrase, You Only Live Once (YOLO) took pop culture by storm. People began using YOLO as an excuse to blow their money, burn relational bridges, and even drink while driving. Nathan A. Heflick, PhD, senior lecturer in psychology at the University of Lincoln in the United Kingdom, wrote about the positive and negative effects of the YOLO mindset. in an article titled "The Psychology of YOLO."

The downside, Heflick penned, includes "reminders of death, of the scarcity of life, often, ironically, promote reckless behavior." The upside is, "When people are aware that life is more scarce, they focus more on positive things, and less on negative things." He continued, "When reminded of death, people become more aware that life is scarce. In turn, this causes people to believe that life is more meaningful."[120] When you think about the fragility of life, how you respond to the truth of life's inevitable ending will dictate your will to cross the starting line. YOLO should urge you to *GO*, not to stop. The fact that you only live once is not an excuse to live reckless but a reason to live responsibly.

1 Reason to Never Stop

When I was in high school, I joined a school club called Generation X. This was a Christian club. The dedication we had to the *cause of Christ* was unique. We prayed at the pole (in front of the school) every morning before school started, then prayed at the pole at the end of every lunch. As if that was not enough prayer, on Mondays, Wednesdays, Thursdays, and Fridays we held a Bible club meeting after school. On Tuesdays, we ran our executive board meetings to discuss the subject matter for the upcoming meetings.

Believe it or not, we did this all year round. Of the many things we learned, something I will never forget is when someone says in our meetings, "You need to live right because some people will never open the Bible. Therefore, your life will be the only Bible people read." That quote shook me to my core. As I pondered it more deeply, I realized the significance and truth behind those words. As a believer, it is imperative to live a genuine life of love, joy, peace, forbearance, kindness, goodness, faithfulness, gentleness and self-control. Not only because that makes God happy but also because that lifestyle is necessary to be a decent and loving person.

Niccolò Machiavelli, an Italian diplomat and philosopher, encouraged a different way of living. He is credited with the phrase "Nice guys finish last." In Machiavelli's book *The Prince*, he encouraged the reader to learn from those who are deceitful, understand how to manipulate, and master how to lead with an iron fist. He believed that the "means justify the ends." In simpler terms, it is okay to do evil with good intentions for a good outcome. Here are some quotes from Niccolò Machiavelli:

> It is imperative to live a genuine life of love, joy, peace, forbearance, kindness, goodness, faithfulness, gentleness and self-control. Not only because that makes God happy but also because that lifestyle is necessary to be a decent and loving person.

"People should either be caressed or crushed. If you do them minor damage they will get their revenge; but if you cripple them there is nothing they can do. If you need to injure someone, do it in such a way that you do not have to fear their vengeance."

"Since love and fear can hardly exist together, if we must choose between them, it is far safer to be feared than loved."[121]

From the moment I heard of Niccolò Machiavelli, I thought about his teachings a lot. I find his methods toward success (or power) are opposite of how I was taught to live. From my experience, the "nice guys finish last" mentality is toxic, partly because I realized that his logic is based on a perceived defeat. In other words, "nice guys" appear to finish last, whereas bad guys seemingly finish first. The non-nice guy may have a better chance at winning the election because they are unafraid to use propaganda and manipulation to win. Or the non-nice guy may be willing to cheat on the final exam to get the best grades while the nice guys study into the night. The non-nice guy (if not caught) will appear to have a divine anointing for success and accolades. They may even become the envy of many who watch from the moral sidelines. In these instances, clearly the nice guy finishes last while everyone who is willing to slither to the top will finish first.

However, the problem with that "Machiavellian" mindset is the "bad" guys are serving everyone else poison so they can appear healthier than everyone else. Little do they know, however, that they are already sick. The damage is done within. Unless the non-nice guy is devoid of a conscience, there are mental, emotional, and spiritual consequences to living without moral borders. Crossing the starting line without a conscience is a social calamity. Not only for the individual but also because of its crippling effect on anyone in its path. All actions taken today, whether negative or positive, will domino into the society of tomorrow.

When pleasure, success, and victory arise from the right foundation, good will be the inevitable result. Dr. King said, "We are caught in an inescapable network of mutuality, tied in a single garment of destiny. Whatever affects one directly, affects all indirectly."[122]

Dear King or Queen, that is one reason to Never Stop.
YOUR ACTIONS MATTER.

From generations past to generations future, every minor decision compounded over time makes significant waves on the direction of this world. When you cross the starting line, you are not alone. You are crossing with your friends, family, and strangers. You are crossing not only for today but also for societies in the future. With that in mind, my dear friend, I implore you to *GO*.

GO with a clean conscious
GO with an open heart
GO with optimism
GO with inspiration
GO with enthusiasm
GO with sincerity
GO with gratitude
GO with courage
GO with grace
GO with joy
GO, with **LOVE.**

GO

Acknowledgements

Thanks a million to everyone for contributing to the success of the book.

Cover Photographer: Paula Augustin

Cover Designer: John Habib

Graphic Designer: Sahara Martin

Book Editor: Book Baby

Many thanks to everyone who read the book and gave feedback before it was complete. Thanks, for the feedback, honestly, and candor. Thanks, Florida International University, for the writing center. To Saif Ishoof for empowering me to read more and think deeper, thank you.

Anne-Marie, thank you for the call you gave me on August 15, 2017 that sparked this book. Thanks, Joshua Senatus for your support morally and financially for the editing of this book. Thanks to my mentors who left a testimonial, Congresswoman Frederica Wilson, Les Standiford, Sho Baraka, and Russell Motley.

Without the never-ending love from my family, none of this would be possible. To Ramces Noel, Marie Noel, David Noël. Makisha Noël, Anderson Noël, I say thanks.

To everyone who helped and supported me in any way, thank you!

I am forever grateful.

Endnotes

[1] "BBC World Service | Learning English | Moving Words." BBC News. http://www.bbc.co.uk/worldservice/learningenglish/movingwords/shortlist/laotzu.shtml.

[2] Hughes, Langston. "Mother to Son by Langston Hughes." Poetry Foundation. https://www.poetryfoundation.org/poems/47559/mother-to-son.

[3] Florida International University - Digital Communications. "Worlds Ahead Graduates." Commencement. https://commencement.fiu.edu/day-of-ceremony/worlds-ahead-graduates/.

[4] "Viktor E. Frankl Quotes (Author of Man's Search for Meaning)." Goodreads. https://www.goodreads.com/author/quotes/2782.Viktor_E_Frankl.

[5] Ibid. p. 19

[6] M, Mateusz. "Mateusz M." Mateusz M. http://www.mateuszm.com/47-motivational-quotes-eric-thomas/.

[7] "BibleGateway." James 1:2-4 NIV - - Bible Gateway. https://www.biblegateway.com/passage/?search=James 1:2-4&version=NIV.

[8] Rigaud, Debbie. "5 Fear-Based Parenting Mistakes I Won't Make." Parents. December 14, 2014. https://www.parents.com/baby/all-about-babies/5-fear-based-parenting-mistakes-i-wont-make/.

[9] Warrell, Margie. "The Antidote For Fear: Focus On What You Want, Not On What You Don't." Forbes. February 05, 2015. https://www.forbes.com/sites/margiewarrell/2015/02/04/layne-beachley-focus-on-what-you-want-not-on-what-you-dont/#3ec850d1d44f.

[10] Covey, Stephen. "Habit 2: Begin With End In Mind." FranklinCovey. https://www.franklincovey.com/the-7-habits/habit-2.html.

[11] Ibid. p. 33

[12] Ghosh, Shikhar. "Why Most Venture-Backed Companies Fail." Harvard Business School. December 10, 2012. https://www.hbs.edu/news/Pages/item.aspx?num=214.

[13] McKinley Irvin. "32 Shocking Divorce Statistics." McKinley Irvin. February 19, 2019. https://www.mckinleyirvin.com/family-law-blog/2012/october/32-shocking-divorce-statistics/.

[14] Weissmann, Jordan. "America's Awful College Dropout Rates, in Four Charts." Slate Magazine. November 19, 2014. https://slate.com/business/2014/11/u-s-college-dropouts-rates-explained-in-4-charts.html.

[15] Rosenberg, Mark B. "During Difficult Times, Panthers Unite." FIU. https://fiustrong.fiu.edu/.

[16] Impelman, Craig. "Never Mistake Activity for Achievement." Coach John Wooden. June 20, 2018. https://www.thewoodeneffect.com/activity-achievement/.

[17] Pelusi, Nando, PhD. "The Lure of Laziness." Psychology Today. July 1, 2007. https://www.psychologytoday.com/us/articles/200707/the-lure-laziness.

[18] Ibid. p. 38

[19] Mertz, Jon. "The Role of Patience in Purpose." Thin Difference. October 13, 2015. https://www.thindifference.com/2015/01/role-patience-purpose/.

[20] Romanov, Nicholas. "Analysis of Usain Bolt's Running Technique." Pose Method. http://www.posemethod.com.cn/usain-bolts-running-technique/.

[21] Hattenstone, Simon. "Usain Bolt: Fast and Loose | Athletics | Simon Hattenstone." The Guardian. August 27, 2010. https://www.theguardian.com/sport/2010/aug/28/usain-bolt-interview.

[22] "Patience | Definition of Patience in English by Lexico Dictionaries." Lexico Dictionaries | English. https://www.lexico.com/en/definition/patience.

[23] "Lazy | Definition of Lazy in English by Lexico Dictionaries." Lexico Dictionaries | English. https://www.lexico.com/en/definition/lazy.

[24] "Rosa Parks." Biography.com. June 24, 2019. https://www.biography.com/activist/rosa-parks.

[25] Hoffman, Bobby, PhD. "Perfectly Wrong: Why Perfection Can Destroy Your Motivation." Psychology Today. July 21, 2017. https://www.psychologytoday.com/us/blog/motivate/201707/perfectly-wrong-why-perfection-can-destroy-your-motivation.

[26] "Michelle Obama: 'I Still Have Impostor Syndrome'." BBC News. December 04, 2018. https://www.bbc.com/news/uk-46434147.

[27] Ibid. p. 48

[28] Swoope, Lawrence Allen, II. "Swoope (Ft. Natalie Lauren) – Best of Me." Genius. August 05, 2014. https://genius.com/Swoope-best-of-me-lyrics.

[29] Lombardi, Vince, Jr. "A Quote by Vince Lombardi Jr." Goodreads. https://www.goodreads.com/quotes/392543-perfection-is-not-attainable-but-if-we-chase-perfection-we.

[30] https://www.youtube.com/watch?v=tVYxvNLsRvs

[31] Noel, Jefferson. "Visionary Paralysis- Eric Thomas 3." YouTube. August 23, 2016. https://www.youtube.com/watch?v=hMQW-

YLnAQ8&list=PLvKE1JkOeAkTSKeLvIeyyWJuCnVrMx20N&index=3.

[32] Kappes, Heather Barry, and Gabriele Oettinhen. "Positive Fantasies about Idealized Futures Sap Energy." Journal of Experimental Social Psychology. February 18, 2011.
http://www.psych.nyu.edu/oettingen/Barry Kappes, H., & Oettingen, G. (2011). JESP.pdf.

[33] "Dale Carnegie." Biography.com. April 15, 2019.
https://www.biography.com/writer/dale-carnegie.

[34] Harvard Health Publishing. "The Health Benefits of Strong Relationships." Harvard Health. December 2010.
https://www.health.harvard.edu/newsletter_article/the-health-benefits-of-strong-relationships.

[35] Quora. "Research Shows Bad Relationships Can Also Mean Bad Health." Forbes. May 03, 2018.
https://www.forbes.com/sites/quora/2018/05/03/research-shows-bad-relationships-can-also-mean-bad-health/#5154f75f1d5e.

[36] Staudenraus, Kim. Kim Staudenraus.
https://www.kimstaudenraus.com/home/.

[37] Zoara. zoara.com. This website is no longer online.

[38] "Compeer | Definition of Compeer in English by Lexico Dictionaries." Lexico Dictionaries | English.
https://www.lexico.com/en/definition/compeer.

[39] "ABOUT US | Mentor Program | 5000 Role Models of Excellence Project | Florida." 5000 Role Models.
https://www.5000rolemodels.com/about-us.

[40] Ibid. p. 66

[41] Noel, Makisha. "Discussion on Mentee." Telephone interview by author. 2018.

[42] BlackPast. "(1904) Mary Church Terrell, "The Progress of Colored Women" • BlackPast." BlackPast. February 01, 2019.
https://www.blackpast.org/african-american-history/1904-mary-church-terrell-progress-colored-women/.

[43] "BibleGateway." 1 Corinthians 15:33 NIV - - Bible Gateway. https://www.biblegateway.com/passage/?search=1 Corinthians 15:33&version=NIV.

[44] Kent, Germany. "A Quote by Germany Kent." Goodreads. https://www.goodreads.com/quotes/8451284-don-t-live-the-same-day-over-and-over-again-and.

[45] Harari, Yuval Noah. "Yuval Noah Harari: "21 Lessons for the 21st Century" @ Talks at Google." Youtube. October 11, 2018. https://www.youtube.com/watch?v=Bw9P_ZXWDJU.

[46] "Objective | Definition of Objective in English by Lexico Dictionaries." Lexico Dictionaries | English. https://www.lexico.com/en/definition/objective.

[47] Kiger, Patrick J. "10 Types of Study Bias." HowStuffWorks Science. March 08, 2018. https://science.howstuffworks.com/life/inside-the-mind/human-brain/10-types-study-bias.htm.

[48] Straub, Kris. "Chainsawsuit by Kris Straub – Now That's What I Call Content." Chainsawsuit by Kris Straub Now Thats What I Call Content. September 16, 2014. http://chainsawsuit.com/comic/2014/09/16/on-research/. The image associated with this citation is fully credited to its creators and publisher.

[49] "Noble | Definition of Noble in English by Lexico Dictionaries." Lexico Dictionaries | English. https://www.lexico.com/en/definition/noble.

[50] "DUTIFUL | Definition in the Cambridge English Dictionary." DUTIFUL | Definition in the Cambridge English Dictionary. https://dictionary.cambridge.org/us/dictionary/english/dutiful.

[51] Sagar. "He Who Says He Can and He Who Says He Can't Are Both Usually Right. – Confucius." Sagar Basak. May 25, 2017. https://sagarbasak.com/he-who-says-he-can-and-he-who-says-he-cant-are-both-usually-right-confucius.

[52] Maxwell, John C. "Making the Transition to Intentional Growth." John Maxwell. September 18, 2012. https://www.johnmaxwell.com/blog/making-the-transition-to-intentional-growth/.

⁵³ Campbell, Celeste, PsyD. "What Is Neuroplasticity?" BrainLine. July 26, 2018. https://www.brainline.org/author/celeste-campbell/qa/what-neuroplasticity.

⁵⁴ Sentis. "Neuroplasticity." YouTube. November 06, 2012. https://www.youtube.com/watch?v=ELpfYCZa87g.

⁵⁵ Talks, TEDx. "After Watching This, Your Brain Will Not Be the Same | Lara Boyd | TEDxVancouver." YouTube. December 15, 2015. https://www.youtube.com/watch?v=LNHBMFCzznE.

⁵⁶ Radparvar, Dave. "Neurons That Fire Together, Wire Together." Holstee. November 26, 2017. https://www.holstee.com/blogs/reflections/neurons-that-fire-together-wire-together.

⁵⁷ Tarell, Sam. "Conversation." Telephone interview by author.

⁵⁸ Harteneck, Patricia. "Breaking Away From Negative Thoughts." Seleni Institute. March 20, 2018. https://www.seleni.org/advice-support/2018/3/20/breaking-away-from-negative-thoughts.

⁵⁹ Ibid. p. 83

⁶⁰ Maraboli, Steve. "A Quote from Unapologetically You." Goodreads. https://www.goodreads.com/quotes/319535-if-you-hang-out-with-chickens-you-re-going-to-cluck.

⁶¹ Capretto, Lisa. "WATCH: Dwyane Wade Says He Was 'Next In Line To Sell Drugs'." HuffPost. May 02, 2013. https://www.huffpost.com/entry/dwyane-wade-childhood-father_n_3196030.

⁶² "EXCUSE | Definition in the Cambridge English Dictionary." EXCUSE | Definition in the Cambridge English Dictionary. https://dictionary.cambridge.org/us/dictionary/english/excuse.

⁶³ Behance, Inc. "99 Excuses For NOT Making Ideas Happen." Adobe 99U. February 27, 2019. https://99u.adobe.com/articles/6842/99-excuses-for-not-making-ideas-happen.

⁶⁴ Brown, Paul B. "'You Miss 100% Of The Shots You Don't Take.' You Need To Start Shooting At Your Goals." Forbes. January 12, 2014. https://www.forbes.com/sites/actiontrumpseverything/2014/01/

12/you-miss-100-of-the-shots-you-dont-take-so-start-shooting-at-your-goal/#7edde3e56a40.

[65] Picasso. "Pablo Picasso Quotes." Brainy Quotes. https://www.brainyquote.com/quotes/pablo_picasso_380469.

[66] Ibid. p. 92 (from citation 62)

[67] Stumm, Sophie Von, Benedikt Hell, and Tomas Chamorro-Premuzic. "The Hungry Mind: Intellectual Curiosity Is the Third Pillar of Academic Performance - Sophie Von Stumm, Benedikt Hell, Tomas Chamorro-Premuzic, 2011." SAGE Journals. October 14, 2011. https://journals.sagepub.com/doi/abs/10.1177/1745691611421204.

[68] American Friends of Tel Aviv University. "Intelligence Is More Accurate Predictor of Future Career Success than Socioeconomic Background, Study Suggests." ScienceDaily. March 29, 2012. https://www.sciencedaily.com/releases/2012/03/120329142035.htm.

[69] Leslie, Ian. "Curious Quotes by Ian Leslie." Goodreads. https://www.goodreads.com/work/quotes/41372439-curious-the-desire-to-know-and-why-your-future-depends-on-it.

[70] Peterson, Jordan B. "12 Rules for Life: London: How To Academy." YouTube. January 30, 2018. https://www.youtube.com/watch?v=PWasTAtR6Ns.

[71] Joubert, Joseph. "A Quote by Joseph Joubert." Goodreads. https://www.goodreads.com/quotes/227289-it-is-better-to-debate-a-question-without-settling-it.

[72] Kassem, Suzy. "A Quote from Rise Up and Salute the Sun." Goodreads. https://www.goodreads.com/quotes/7387466-i-have-been-finding-treasures-in-places-i-did-not.

[73] "Luke 14." Bible Hub. Accessed June 28, 2019. https://biblehub.com/luke/14-28.htm.

[74] "Student Loan Resources: Financial Aid & Loan Debt Management." Debt.org. 2018. https://www.debt.org/students/.

[75] Carnevale, Anthony P., Stephen J. Rose, and Ban Cheah. "S The College Payoff: Education, Occupations, Lifetime Earnings." The College Payoff. https://1gyhoq479ufd3yna29x7ubjn-wpengine.netdna-ssl.com/wp-content/uploads/2014/11/collegepayoff-summary.pdf.

[76] Noel, Jefferson. "Caution: The Road to Purpose Is Slippery." Jefferson Noel. March 19, 2019. https://jeffersonnoel.com/2017/11/22/caution-road-purpose-slippery/.

[77] "Opposition Research | Definition of Opposition Research in English by Lexico Dictionaries." Lexico Dictionaries | English. https://www.lexico.com/en/definition/opposition_research.

[78] M, Mateusz. "Dream - Motivational Video." YouTube. July 02, 2013. https://www.youtube.com/watch?v=g-jwWYX7Jlo.

[79] Council, Forbes Coaches. "Can't Figure Out Your Passion? Ask Yourself These 14 Questions." Forbes. June 04, 2018. https://www.forbes.com/sites/forbescoachescouncil/2018/06/04/cant-figure-out-your-passion-ask-yourself-these-14-questions/#214601550c06.

[80] United Methodist Communications. "What Is Aldersgate Day?" The United Methodist Church. May 12, 2015. http://www.umc.org/what-we-believe/what-is-aldersgate-day.

[81] "Marking John Wesley's Birthday in His Words." United Methodist News Service. June 28, 2012. https://www.umnews.org/en/news/marking-john-wesleys-birthday-in-his-words.

[82] Zacharias, Ravi. "Cries of The Heart." Google Books. https://books.google.com/books?id=6rGmC_V63F8C&pg=PA48&lpg=PA48&dq=john wesley Laziness is slowly creeping in. There is an increasing tendency to stay in bed after five-thirty in the morning."&source=bl&ots=0tQq95lyPf&sig=ACfU3U2uGj_AuASBrT5OLs61HVuUjMw_Sg&hl=en&sa=X&ved=2ahUKEwiB64OurI3jAhUEwlkKHVfRDrMQ6AEwAnoECAkQAQ#v=onepage&q=john wesley Laziness is slowly creeping in. There is an

increasing tendency to stay in bed after five-thirty in the morning."&f=false.

[83] "Ellen Johnson Sirleaf Quotes (Author of This Child Will Be Great)." Goodreads. Accessed June 29, 2019. https://www.goodreads.com/author/quotes/2116089.Ellen_Johnson_Sirleaf.

[84] Hansen, Drew. "Steve Jobs On Misfit Entrepreneurs." Forbes. August 19, 2011. https://www.forbes.com/sites/drewhansen/2011/08/01/steve-jobs-on-misfit-entrepreneurs/#212ee1be72f7.

[85] "Conversation about Power Steps vs. Baby Steps." Telephone interview by author.

[86] Allan, Patrick. ""Don't Confuse Motion and Progress"." Lifehacker. January 07, 2015. https://lifehacker.com/dont-confuse-motion-and-progress-1678075284.

[87] "A Quote by Dalai Lama XIV." Goodreads. https://www.goodreads.com/quotes/7777-if-you-think-you-are-too-small-to-make-a.

[88] "Mosquitoes." National Geographic. September 24, 2018. https://www.nationalgeographic.com/animals/invertebrates/group/mosquitoes/.

[89] Rettner, Rachael. "The Weight of the World: Researchers Weigh Human Population." LiveScience. June 17, 2012. https://www.livescience.com/36470-human-population-weight.html.

[90] "Mosquito Facts." Prairie Research Institute. http://www.inrs.illinois.edu/expo/pdf-files/mosquito-facts.pdf.

[91] Shaw, George Bernard. ""I Want to Be Thoroughly Used up When I Die." -- George Bernard Shaw on Taking Creative Action." Rebelle Society. January 09, 2017. http://www.rebellesociety.com/2013/08/23/i-want-to-be-all-used-up-when-i-die-george-bernard-shaw-on-taking-creative-action/.

[92] Cherry, Kendra. "How the Status Quo Bias Influences the Decisions You Make." Verywell Mind. June 14, 2019.

https://www.verywellmind.com/status-quo-bias-psychological-definition-4065385.

93 Ibid. p. 128

94 "About Me." L'union Suite. https://www.lunionsuite.com/about/.

95 Tan, Chris. "The Chinese Bamboo Tree – Les Brown Motivational Speech." Motivation Mentalist. December 04, 2018. https://motivationmentalist.com/2018/07/23/chinese-bamboo-tree-les-brown-motivational-speech/.

96 TEDxYouth. "Financial Literacy: Mellody Hobson at TEDxMidwest." YouTube. March 11, 2014.
https://www.youtube.com/watch?v=h9o5Zx7m4Fs.

97 "BibleGateway." Zechariah 4:10 NLT - - Bible Gateway.
https://www.biblegateway.com/passage/?search=Zechariah 4:10&version=NLT.

98 "LeBron James." Wikipedia.
https://en.wikipedia.org/wiki/LeBron_James.

99 "A Quote by Theodore Roosevelt." Goodreads.
https://www.goodreads.com/quotes/7-it-is-not-the-critic-who-counts-not-the-man.

100 Covey, Stephen R. The 7 Habits of Highly Effective People Wisdom and Insight. Philadelphia: Running Press, 1989. Page 219

101 Lesliejosephs. "Travelers Paid Airlines a Record $4.6 Billion Last Year to Check Their Luggage." CNBC. May 07, 2018.
https://www.cnbc.com/2018/05/07/travelers-paid-airlines-a-record-4-point-6-billion-in-bag-fees-in-2017.html.

102 Karavbrandeisky. "The Best (and Worst) Airline Baggage Fees." MONEY.com. March 16, 2016.
http://money.com/money/collection-post/4257971/best-travel-airline-baggage-fees/.

103 Ibid. p. 160

104 Bloom, Linda, and Charlie Bloom. "Beware of Corporate Marriage Syndrome." Psychology Today. July 22, 2018.
https://www.psychologytoday.com/us/blog/stronger-the-broken-places/201807/beware-corporate-marriage-syndrome.

105 Ibid. p. 164

[106] "A Story About Integrity: "The New Emperor"." Management Training Resources. http://www.managetrainlearn.com/page/the-new-emperor.

[107] Spoon, Alan. "What 'Pivot' Really Means." Inc.com. August 10, 2012. https://www.inc.com/alan-spoon/what-pivot-really-means.html.

[108] Acharya, Debi. "Anything in Excess Is Bad." Speakingtree.in. January 20, 2014. https://www.speakingtree.in/blog/anything-in-excess-is-bad.

[109] Ibid. p. 171

[110] "Ravi Zacharias: A Lecherous Heart." Sermon Central. November 27, 2010. https://www.sermoncentral.com/sermon-illustrations/77711/ravi-zacharias-a-lecherous-heart-by-gordon-curley.

[111] Katz, David J. "Everything That Can Be Invented Has Been Invented - The Startup." Medium. June 4, 2015. https://medium.com/swlh/everything-that-can-be-invented-has-been-invented-49c4376f548b.

[112] Danelek, Jeff. "What Are the Most Important Inventions of the 20th Century." Toptenz.net. September 9, 2010. https://www.toptenz.net/top-10-inventions-of-the-20th-century.php.

[113] Extremegrowth8, and Les Brown. "Les Brown You Gotta Be Hungry." YouTube. July 30, 2013. https://www.youtube.com/watch?v=pyHMRwrS1pc.

[114] Khaled, Khaled Mohamed. "A Quote by D.J. Khaled." Goodreads. https://www.goodreads.com/quotes/7412093-they-don-t-want-you-to-win.

[115] "Social Comparison Theory." Psychology Today. https://www.psychologytoday.com/us/basics/social-comparison-theory.

[116] "How Fast Is the Earth Moving?" Scientific American. https://www.scientificamerican.com/article/how-fast-is-the-earth-mov/.

[117] "A Quote by Dwight D. Eisenhower." Goodreads. https://www.goodreads.com/quotes/48124-the-history-of-free-men-is-never-written-by-chance.

[118] Goldsmith, Marshall. What Got You Here, Won't Get You There. Page 184

[119] https://www.goodreads.com/quotes/21045-if-a-man-is-called-to-be-a-street-sweeper

[120] Heflick, Nathan A., PhD. "The Psychology of "YOLO"." Psychology Today. September 21, 2013. https://www.psychologytoday.com/us/blog/the-big-questions/201309/the-psychology-yolo.

[121] "Niccolò Machiavelli Quotes (Author of The Prince)." Goodreads. https://www.goodreads.com/author/quotes/16201.Niccol_Machiavelli

[122] "Letter from a Birmingham Jail [King, Jr.]." Letter from a Birmingham Jail [King, Jr.]. https://www.africa.upenn.edu/Articles_Gen/Letter_Birmingham.html

Thank you for reading!

Author's Abridged Bio:

Jefferson Noel is a young Haitian-American community educator, born and raised in Miami, FL. He has written numerous articles online, published his book "Powerful Presenting: How to Overcome One of the Nation's Greatest Fears" in December 2017 and his most recent book, GO: How to Cross the Starting Line. Jefferson founded Barbershop Speaks— an organization dedicated to engaging in intelligent discussions inside Barbershops and Beauty Salons to enlighten, educate, and empower the community. Jefferson has been featured on MSNBC, NBC News Now, WSVN, NPR, WLRN, NBC 6, Aventura News, The South Florida Times, The Haitian Times, and the Miami Times. He is experienced in the areas of Public Speaking, Servant Leadership, Education, and Entrepreneurship. His efforts in the community led him to receive the Revolutionary Leadership Award, Outstanding Service Award by FIU, New Generation of Dreamers, the Young Adult Action Award by HANA, The Young Professional Haitian- American Top 20 Under 40 distinction, the Legacy of Leadership Award, the Raul Moncarz Award of Excellence, and many more awards and recognitions. He is a distinguished World's Ahead graduate from Florida International University with a Bachelors in Communications and a Master's degree in Global Strategic Communication with a certificate in Conflict Resolution. Jefferson is the past President of the Student Government at Florida International University-BBC, former member of FIU Foundation Board, and past chairman of the Mental Health committee with the Florida Student Association which is a governing body of twelve state universities that comprise of four hundred thousand students. Jefferson is currently a professor at Florida Memorial University.

www.ingramcontent.com/pod-product-compliance
Lightning Source LLC
Chambersburg PA
CBHW030433010526
44118CB00011B/623